THE
LIFE
BALANCE
PROGRAMME

THE
LIFE
BALANCE
PROGRAMME

A POWERFUL STRATEGY FOR COMBINING PERSONAL FULFILMENT AND CAREER SUCCESS

PETA LYN FARWAGI

ORION
BUSINESS
BOOKS

To Morwenna, the beautiful daughter and friend I am so fortunate to have in my life.

The right of Peta Lyn Farwagi to be identified as the author of this work has been asserted by her in accordance with the Copyright, Designs and Patents Act 1988.

This edition first published in Great Britain in 1998 by
Orion Business
An imprint of The Orion Publishing Group Ltd
Orion House, 5 Upper St Martin's Lane, London WC2H 9EA

A CIP catalogue record for this book
is available from the British Library.

ISBN 0-75281-367-6

Designed by Leigh Jones
Illustrations © Ceri Staziker
Printed and bound in Great Britain by
Butler & Tanner Ltd, Frome and London

CONTENTS

Acknowledgements vi

Introduction 1

PART 1
IDENTIFYING YOUR OWN SITUATION 7
1 Balance Comes First 9
2 Balancing Your Dreams 25
3 Balance Amid the Turbulence 31
4 Balancing Your Environment 39
5 Balancing the Future 48

PART 2
SORTING OUT YOUR PAST AND
LOOKING AT YOUR FUTURE 59
6 Balancing Influences 61
7 Balancing the Past and the Future 94

PART 3
FINDING THE CENTRE POINT OF YOUR WORLD 109
8 Balancing the Inner and Outer You 111
9 Balancing You and Your Place in the Bigger Picture 116

PART 4
THE BUILDING PROCESS:
SETTING IN A STEADY BALANCE 121
10 Balancing Different Rhythms 123
11 Balancing Your Financial Expectations 136
12 Balancing Your Network 145
13 Balancing Home and Office 150
14 Balancing Your Time 160
15 Staying in Balance 165

ACKNOWLEDGEMENTS

I want to acknowledge Martin Liu, Publishing Director of Orion Business, who suggested I write this book and then was a marvellously intelligent and quietly supportive person to work with. Whenever I talked with him I always felt my spirits lift.

At Orion too, Clare Christian, who saw that every little detail was in place.

I want to thank my clients, who are part of the foundation of this book. They trusted me with their lives and gave me joy when I saw them move ahead in their own ways with the ideas and plans we worked on together.

Also my friends, whether mentioned by name or not, because they have been an integral part of my understandings on the balance of my life.

INTRODUCTION

To start to write The Life Balance Programme as a book I went to stay in an old country house hotel in the south of England, set in a huge curved bay, with high rocky headlands either end and an expanse of sea, the perfect place for a mind's adventure. At the end of the first afternoon I walked in the mist along the wet rocks and beach, wondering just how I would begin.

I hadn't been to Cornwall since I was a child and I had a wonderful childish time this adult afternoon, skipping to get away from the waves, throwing flat flinty rocks to skim with my joy along the grey flat surfaces between the incoming white swells. I remembered the hopeful dreams I had recited to myself as a sturdy, roundish, defiant, audacious eleven-year-old. Here I had walked the cliffs for hours and hours to get away from the treacherously emotional atmosphere that was our rented home every year for the month of August.

This recent afternoon I knew clearly that this had to be a different kind of writing than any I had done before. To convey what I wanted

to say to you I was going to have to write about myself. To communicate my ideas, I would have to explain to you how I had got here. Fear
rushed in like another wave. My heart expanded, my rib-cage
stretched. My mouth opened and I was suddenly yelling out loud on
the wind, Heeeeeeeelllllp!

The yell went on for an eerily long time, echoing against the cliffs
and through my ears with a vibrancy that ended with a new, unfamiliar kind of strength. In this strength I knew why I could write about
myself now. My own life had started to come into a deeper level of balance. I had always found it easy to run around the world, to keep the
balance I needed to interview people and come back and write descrip-
tively about what and whom I saw, whether Papua New Guinea,
Borneo, New York or Joan Sutherland in the boardroom of the Sydney
Opera House; whether for *Vogue*, the *Australian* or the *London Business
School Magazine*. But the times I had tried to sit down and write about
my life had always been too frightening; being still with myself was
extremely difficult and just too painful. When I stopped for too long I
would remember that inside I felt as if I was not good enough.

I understood, in the calm after this horizon-stretching yell, the
tricks I had played to stop myself from feeling a long-carried hurt of
not being heard at home. I had, without knowing it, allowed a surface
fear to stop me at the first painful emotional level. And to help me cut
off from the hurt lying under that fear, I had simply registered a belief-
system in my mind that I was boring. I must be, otherwise why would-
n't anyone listen to me when I was a child, and if they did sometimes
listen to me because I occasionally got brave and demanded it, why
did they laugh at my attempts to talk about my young passion, the
world around us?

That day on a wild and empty beach I understood that because I
had, over the last seven years, brought myself into this new equilibrium, I would now have my own balanced self as an anchor to hold
on to as I went diving deep inside for these words. I had a new sense
of completeness, that the inner me was now in balance with the outer
me. As I thought about this I knew I was safe in this new, deeply
placed, happily balanced life-position.

Because I had found this new spring-water-clear equilibrium, the
pool of past hurt I had protected suddenly didn't matter any more. I
could see that the pain that as a child I had fearfully imagined was

going to extinguish me was really just a small bundle of hurt to an adult, something I could now yell away on a wild sea.

I started to skip along the beach, all fifty-three years of me skipping like a five-year-old. When I am working with my clients on their *Life Strategies,* I often ask the more serious and high-level ones to skip, particularly those who carry the responsibility of running organisations. It is hard to keep your good spirits down when you skip – everything bounces, shakes and lightens. I usually end up laughing at myself. I remind and remind my clients until they give into my whim. When they have skipped they always laugh when they tell me about it. This afternoon my laughter followed that yell and it felt like a nice symmetry

I had always to be aware during my fastest-moving, round-the-world times to keep in balance the intimate and the greater scheme of things. Because I have been such a loner on my travels, in those phases when I was a teenage ice-skater or travel editor for Vogue, when I also had my own family of husband and child, I had to learn to shift myself regularly between two very different kinds of life. I became quite adept at this as I moved and worked through seventy-odd countries and maintained a happy home.

I have also fallen out of balance a few times, once very painfully. When I left Australia in 1992, after ten years living in Sydney, I lost my balance altogether for a while. I changed too much at once. I left my marriage, my work, my own office, sold my home, sold fifty-five boxes of books and my furniture. My daughter decided to take a gap year before university so she stayed in Australia; therefore, for the first time in nineteen years, I was without family. On my way back to this next stage of my life in the UK, I worked in Africa for four months, in war zones and Aids areas.

When I finally arrived in England, I decided to do the London Business School's Sloan Fellowship, a fellowship which also runs at Stratford and MIT. I found a temporary flat and plunged in. That year, studying in a class of fifty-two senior-level executives from all around the world taking a sabbatical, was quite stressfully challenging. When I graduated, there were no family in England to see me in my gown. When I finished the course I decided to start a new career. Not content to add the new skills to my old ones, as I had intended, I hungered for something different. I had always been good at change I thought, I can do this again. I was teetering in a totally alien world. So, what did I do but invent a new career. I designed one for myself, to work with career people on their *Life Strategies*.

What was I thinking of? I had stripped myself bare. How could I stay sane, let alone in any kind of balance. At times I found it hard to recognise myself at all. I lost the high level of health I had gained through my upbringing, got exhausted and became rather emotional. My body hurt all over. I couldn't see balance, didn't even see I was out of it. It was like sitting in a pot of hot oil. And every time I tried to get out I just fell back in. Ouch.

During my year as a Sloan I was the one who kept reminding people about their 'real lives', the world outside the London Business School, that they had emotions they needed to be considering alongside the international strategic management, new markets and company culture, that business wasn't the only reason for life. I kept filling already over-stuffed pigeon holes with challenging personal quotes.

I could see that my fellow participants were actually having as much trouble with the change that this sabbatical year was bringing into their mid-career lives as they were with subjects such as finance and marketing. I was concerned for the other fifty-one participants, but because it was all so absorbing I didn't realise quite what was happening to me.

When I left and added the new career to all this change I added more stress. I got thinner and thinner. I ran out of energy and felt exhausted. One of my acquaintances started to make jokes about mid-life anorexia. It was all a little frightening. Why couldn't I cope, I kept asking myself, I'm so strong, I'm one of the strongest people I know.

I started to look back on my life for explanations, for the times I had loved, for the moments I felt best. I realised in doing this that to start my new career I had to regain that sure balance I had taken for granted. There were other questions: How was I going to get my strength back? How was I going to remind my life-print, my inner codes, that they had been pretty good at balance before this crisis? And how was I going to set in this life balance so that I would never lose it again? How was I going to build myself a solid new future that would also have room for the unexpected? How could I be sure, when I hit another difficult time, I would move through it with equilibrium?

I wanted to find one person who could look at my whole life with me. I talked to therapists, health practitioners, spiritualists, body-workers, energy balancers, business consultants, human resource directors, leading international London Business School professors, artists, scientists, archaeologists and writers. Each of them had an opinion and I didn't find it easy to reconcile all these points of view. I know that's the quest of a lifetime but I remember saying to a friend about ten years ago, I just want a very wise old person to sit beside. I haven't found one, although I have talked to many inspiring people around the world.

I worked out a step-by-step process and built it into a programme. I based it on the work I had done in ice-skating, experiential psychology, publishing, business, interviewing people around the world and the health and medical background from several generations of my father's family. It is this process, together with this background, that I offer my clients.

The purpose of creating *Life Strategies* was to work with people across the whole spectrum of their lives. I'm not yet old enough to be that very wise person I longed for but I have journeyed through many countries and many disciplines, learned many disparate skills and probably explored more avenues than most sensible people know exist. I have asked a million questions, probably more. Sometimes in the darkness of looking for the answers, I have been reassured by remembering my intrepid and quietly brave grandmother's reassuring voice: 'Peta Lyn, you were born with a question mark carved on your forehead, you will travel far.' Because of this journey I have garnered the skills I pass on to you here.

I decided to write a book on this search for a new balance because whenever my clients come to me to plan their *Life Strategies* we always spend as much time working out how to balance their lives as they move ahead to the new as we do on planning the new. I remember my first client, George Bain, then principal of the London Business School, sitting down opposite me at the first session in his large, august study looking out on to London's Regent Park. Having originally given me a brief to help him decide whether he should take another term at the school, he suddenly asked me with need, 'In this job, my life has become ninety per cent work and that leaves ten per cent for everything else. Can you change that?'

To help me advise Bain, I had in my tool-kit the example of one of my dearest friends, film-maker Peter Weir, director of *Witness*, who, at the height of his first real success in Hollywood, turned his back on the movie-making system and went home for a year off to build a garden for his new home overlooking an inland sea north of Sydney. I asked Peter why he would do this at this high and risky point. 'I want to be making films in my eighties and if I don't take the time to stop now I will burn out long before.' The year wasn't always easy; suddenly changing rhythms never is. But it was high wisdom from a then thirty-something.

This book is about the successes and the mistakes I made finding my way back to a balanced state. It is also about my clients, their careers and the discoveries they have made. As I wrote it, I gained a deeper and deeper sense of balance for myself. As I went through the ideas I wanted to give you, I felt progressively a little happier, a little more solid, a little more joyous – I settled in to feeling more and more serene.

I have written *The Life Balance Programme* as a four-part, fifteen-stage programme so that you can read the whole programme in one or refer to the different stages as you first need them or as you need to be reminded of them after you have achieved balance. The last stage, Chapter Fifteen covers, in brief form, what is in the whole book and gives you a simple, clear list to check in and out of as time goes by.

What I want for you, as you work through the book, is to achieve the same ultimate outcome I have, but in your own context. As well as consolidating the deeper sense of balance I have already mentioned, writing the book brought me to an unexpected crossroads and gave me the opportunity to fundamentally reshape my route ahead.

PART 1

IDENTIFYING YOUR OWN SITUATION

In this first part of the programme you find the questions that will trigger you to identify your own particular situation. You will recognise where you are right now and what you need to be aware of to set yourself on a new and balanced path. You consider your dreams, understand the turbulence around you and look at the exponentially fast-changing environment you live in.

This first section helps you to stand back and take stock, to start to draw the line between work and personal life. When you have thought through these essentials, you will be firmly set on a powerful strategic path to combining personal fulfilment and career success.

CHAPTER ONE

BALANCE COMES FIRST

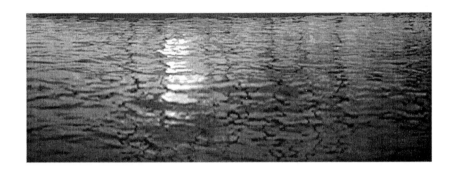

T his chapter is the most challenging. I want you to understand
what your life looks like. Here you look at the dance of balance of
which we are all a part and find answers to life's difficult questions
– what is this life you have and what do you really want to do with it?
You work out where you are out of control and see that building balance
into your life is the basis for long-term success in your career.

What is this life thing you have? On this planet we know that we are born and we die. We know that in this gap of time we are given flesh, bones, genes, emotions, possibilities, opportunities, consciousness and a set of restrictions that others before us have set out. We don't know too much else, although we may wonder about aliens, gods, the spirit, the afterlife and the future of homo-cyberneticus dreamed up in places like Mr Gates' Seattle lakeside-campus and British Telecom's highly experimental Martlesham Research Laboratory in the UK.

This certainty, this life thing, the certain bit between birth and death, that each of us owns exclusively, carries an awesome individual responsibility with it, that we each make the best of it and we each in our lives contribute something that helps to keep our corner of the universe in a balanced state for the next generations.

Our human world doesn't change much from generation to generation; we still do all the same human things, we just put a new language on them. We still have all the same human qualities as cave beings, Genghis Kahn or Ghandi, although like these rather different examples, we may individually use some of them more at one time than at others. Looking back on my own life, for instance, there have been phases when I had huge amounts of courage and phases, one for seven years, where my courage went to the bottom of the list of qualities available to me.

The other certainty we have is that our planet, our galaxy and our universe are all perfectly poised in a dance of balance that keeps each of us precisely positioned in the greater scheme of things. From a particle or atom in one cell of us to every other particle or atom in the universe since the big bang – that is, everything we see around us, which make up this dance of balance – we are, each of us, holding our place in the same gigantic balancing pattern.

And if we inherently understand, in our very cells, this dance of balance, why don't we use this skill in a more focused way to make our lives healthier, wealthier and wiser? We have, sitting inside us, this balance skill, and it is all we need to make of our lives what we will. It is ours. It is free. It is an awesomely untapped strength, which it is time we brought higher on our list of competencies.

Your innate sense of place in the scene of things is the wider context of feeling that you are in balance and as you work your way through the whole *life balance programme* you will develop this balance skill. You will find, as you work this way with your life, that you can tap a more powerful strength than you knew was there. As you bring this strength higher on your list of competencies you will notice that the people around you start to vote with your voice.

The narrower context, the one you can see every day but is still part of the same holding pattern, is all the pieces of your immediate life you feel better about when you have them sharply in focus. These pieces, such as the blurring of divisions between work and your personal life, are the ones that bring so much stress. They are the ones that, when you have them in perspective, set you into the best balance between personal fulfilment and career success.

In the high-pressured business environment, where it is often almost impossible to keep control over your life, you will get the outcomes you want if you keep this whole picture at the foundation of your thinking. As you work your way through the programme it will become clearer and clearer that life balance, living in balance, is taking control over your place in this gigantic holding pattern.

Think, for a moment, of the times you have been in a balancing position, canoeing on a lake, climbing a mountain, white-water rafting. Put yourself into that position and remember how you felt whether perched precariously on high or wobbling perilously through a turbulent patch of water. Everything in you is working together. You are drawing on everything you have to get through this experience. You feel frightened, exhilarated, inspired. You are caught up in this moment of challenge, at one with yourself. Your personal resources are working for the perfect balance you need to deal with this moment. You have total clarity. You are sitting at the centre of yourself, at your Centre Point, and you are in clear communication with the forces around you.

Now think of another of these kind of moments in your life, a less dramatic one, perhaps the one that made you buy this book, and ask yourself how far you are off this sense of balance. Ask yourself how effectively you are using your personal resources to keep your day-to-day in balance. Now look at the world around you; are you in balance with it?

WHAT DOES YOUR LIFE LOOK LIKE? WHAT IS YOUR LIFE-PRINT?

Just in case my clients are taking their day-to-day life too seriously, and most of them are, I ask them to draw a picture of their lives. I give them pen and paper, a large blank sheet, and I watch. Most freeze, some smile, giggle, or look at me as though they are sitting in front of a mad woman. A Chairman of an oil services company protests, 'But I never think in pictures, I have an engineer's mind.' I explain that it's OK, whatever they do, I have been drawn anything from a helicopter to a scrawl. They often say they can't draw. I say neither can I and it doesn't matter, this isn't a skill test, it's just a quick impression of how you see your life.

In a class at INSEAD, one of the top business schools in Europe, at Fontainbleau, outside Paris, I almost had a collective rejection when I asked the participants to do this; but coaxing is something I know how to do and we soon had three of these senior executives drawing their own life-prints on the three boards. One drew a large pillar, another a scrawl with tiny hearts off to the side, the third an aeroplane with arrows going both ways. There was much laughter around the class-room and the rest eagerly set about drawing their own life-prints. One of the things the class quickly noticed was that all three people had left out themselves. So, when it came to making decisions about their lives, they were not putting themselves anywhere near first; certainly the scale in the balance of their lives was heavily tipped to work. They had got to the point that they almost didn't have a physical reality, they were almost an idea associated with their work.

The reason I ask for this drawing is that we hold our lives in our heads or in places like the financial sheets of our computers and we go round and round the same ideas. Heads are not great managers; we are not objective enough with them. Heads hold long-known patterns that we run along happily or unhappily. One of the main reasons we become overloaded or out of balance is because we keep running through these tired, burnt out rat runs and it hurts. The financial sheets in our computers, wonderfully organising as they are, with their *'what if'* scenarios, are still an extension of the way we think and, therefore, very much under our control.

With a quick visual, you can bypass immediately the way you mentally perceive your life and get in under the defences. Draw one and you take the first step towards realising where you are out of balance. The scrawl shown below with two tiny hearts somewhere out to the side comes from a woman who works, has two children and a husband in a high-intensity international consultancy. She wants more time for the heart stuff but is stuck in running here, there and everywhere. She was appalled at her own drawing but when she could see it in front of her it wasn't hard to get her to start to change.

The drawing overleaf of the point with the lines radiating out comes from a man who runs a company. He has a wife whom he adores but she is one of the things he compartmentalises. He feels lonely and isolated juggling the compartments. But it didn't occur to him until he saw it in front of him, just what he was doing.

If you didn't immediately stop to do your own drawing, do it now. Take no longer than two minutes, any longer and you will think too much about it. Just get a visual down on paper. Then look at it carefully for a few minutes, writing down the opposites of what you see there. If everything is cramped together, for instance, work out what you need to do to open it up. If you are at the centre of everything in your life, as shown in the illustration overleaf, then think what you need to do to share some of the roles you have. If you aren't in the drawing at all, draw it again, with you in it and see how that changes the way you see your life.

How often have you avoided making a bold, brave move, just because you were afraid of something new? Are you putting in long

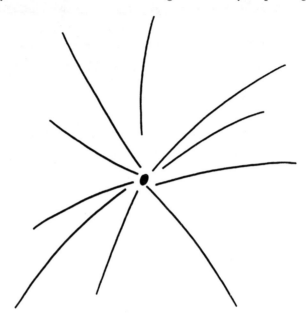

hours at work but suspect you are not really achieving anything of lasting worth? Would you like to spend more time with your friends and family, or to pursue long-held dreams? Was this meant to be the year you finally got fit, or finished that half-written novel you shoved in a drawer too long ago? Do you feel too exhausted to even pick up a book - let alone write one? If these types of questions show up in your drawing and you see that you are caught in some kind of trap, then the drawing has been useful.

A clear example of this is the drawing opposite. The young man I was working with, who had been studying and working in the medical and psychiatric disciplines for twelve years, said rather ruefully when he saw what he had drawn, 'I didn't realise I was nearly drowning, and to think that I feel the sun is setting on me at thirty.' He had come to discuss a career change, perhaps a move to financial services where he would earn more money.

In the first session we discussed his life generally and I explained to him that before he went out and changed his career he needed to fill himself up - he had been giving out and giving out until he had noth-

ing left to give. What he didn't see was that he had fallen out of balance. Logically he couldn't see a reason to change course in his life, although his whole being was saying, 'This is enough, I can't take this any more.' He was still doing a good job: 'I think the people in the hospital would be surprised if I say I am leaving.'

But a recent holiday of three weeks hadn't lifted his spirits; he had spent a lot of money, used most of his holiday allowance, and this drawing was visual evidence that he was even more unhappy than he had realised. He was, as my grandmother would have put it, beside himself with worry. He was empty, his energy was attached to everyone he was trying to fix, he had given too much of himself away.

We set him a programme of things to do that were entirely different from his normal, rather interior, institutionalised way of living and working. We shifted the balance. Instead of looking inside himself and looking inside other people, I wanted him to go hiking so that he could look at horizons, learn how to fly or scuba dive (his to be the choice) so that he would move into another dimension. We perceive our lives very differently when we stand on a Himalayan hilltop or float around in the quiet of the sea's depths. I asked him to put squash aside for a while because it was another interior pursuit.

We also included a massage every two weeks, so that his body was looked after and so that he received some energy from someone else for a change. This would allow him to start balancing what he had given out. He was to put more time into inspirational pursuits, such as going to concerts and looking at paintings. He had forgotten to dance in his life, and, therefore, lost his inherent dance of balance.

A lot to learn from one drawing? This drawing is the life-print you carry around with you, even if you are not aware of it. Start to change it and you will change your everyday behaviour with very little effort. Later in the book I will ask for more drawings and these will be your new life-prints. Once you have installed these new ones in your mind, you will start to operate from a more positive base.

Life-prints are rather like fingerprints. The difference is that you can see finger-prints and someone outside your life can identify you by reading them. Your life-print is your own identity but you cannot actually see it; it is your identify as you understand it, your life as you know it at any given moment. It is how you feel about the way you are and the way you run your life.

Sitting here, writing this, I wondered what my own is; for some reason it is the only part of the *Life Strategies* process I haven't tried on myself. I scribbled it quickly and I half laughed and half cried. I drew a sky-scraper building with me on the face of it, about a third of the way up, climbing to the top. I recognise this. I never stop challenging myself. But part of me says, 'Oh, Peta Lyn, it is enough, stop. How many more mountains do you want to climb? Isn't three careers enough for one life?' Then I smile a little because I remember I have reached a more secure place. But I haven't taken the time to change my life-print, so I do keep reverting to the same trigger thinking. The ease of life I have built since my huge change in 1992 needs a new picture, so I can dance my balance with awareness and ease.

When you are looking for balance in your life, play with the opposites of what you already do. I was having trouble persuading Businesswoman of the Year Prue Leith to empty her diary enough to allow space for the next stage of her life. 'But I find it so hard to say no.' I asked her to say no to everything for a week, just for the experience. 'You can say yes five minutes later if you want, but get used to saying no.'

'I can't,' she said, 'everyone will think I've gone mad.' I suggested they wouldn't even notice. A week later she came back, grinning ruefully. 'They didn't notice.' Prue's life-print was that she was always busy, always had more to do than the time allotted, although her efficiency and that of her two secretaries always carried her through. We had let some air into her closely packed life-print and she began to have room for some new futures.

TOOLS

- Draw what you think your life looks like right now. Take one to two minutes.

- Keep referring to this drawing as you go through the book. Notice how you change this first life-print as you go through the programme.

BALANCE COMES FIRST, YOUR CAREER COMES SECOND

When I say that having balance in your life comes before your career you may think I expect you to put on a pair of Jesus sandals, chant and take less notice of your career. That's not it. What I am saying is that unless you sort out the balance issues, make sure you are safely on an even keel and plot the way ahead to keep yourself there in times of change or crisis, you will often find your career difficult, a threat, overwhelming.

I often see people who have reached a point of no return in their careers because they have tried harder and harder, put in more and more time to succeed and then just run out of their ability to survive in our fast-moving world.

These people, sometimes with a sigh or relief, fall out of their chosen careers into something else, such as being a massage therapist. Ah, they say, this is a softer world, this is more supportive, I will be amongst gentler people. The trouble is that the contrast is so big they don't make a success of the new work either. First, because they may have made too big a change and it takes a long time to adapt through a major change. Second, because they haven't worked out the new balance issues. It is just as easy to get stressed being a massage therapist as it is being a finance director if you haven't got the balance of your life, your balance mechanism, in good order.

Knowing that we are balanced – calm when we need to be, exhilarated when we want to be, our lives containing the elements or components we want and need – has to lie at the centre of us. We are brought up from childhood to believe at a very base-level that we can't have what we want. It is not our parents fault; there were lots of things that weren't practical for us to have and they told us so, in no uncertain terms. As babies we knew we wanted safety, warmth, cuddles and some yummy food. After a while safety disappeared, warmth was much less frequent, cuddles sometimes arrived in the form of spanks, yummy food somehow deteriorated into spinach and carrots. Why couldn't we stay with what was sooooo good?

It is a useful exercise to sit quietly and try to remember the feeling you had sitting in your cot or pram, of being safe, of knowing what your body felt like, of sensing safety all round you, of feeling good-will going out naturally from you and coming towards you on all sides. I don't want to dress up senior executives in nappies, but remembering that feeling, that sense of absolute well-being, is a useful bit of your history to have at your command.

If you have just taken a knock, been made redundant or had something happen that seems life-threatening, going back to a period when you felt entirely safe helps. Your life was balanced back then, so use that early life-print to improve the current one.

The accepted convention we live with is that we have to bow down to career's demands. That we have to give up so much of our lives to earn the money we want and need. We tend to sit in an all-or-nothing framework of career comes first, extras afterwards, in the time left. We think that, unless we get our careers spot on and put all our energies into it, we will not succeed. We think it is a different case for artists or very creative people, but it is important to realise that we all have an inner artist, increasingly so as technology allows us to broaden our lives and our knowledge.

The reality is quite the reverse from our career-first attitudes. Building balance into your life is the basis for long-term success in your career. The people who don't fall over, get over-stressed or have to leave jobs because of personality conflicts are the ones who have taken time to figure out a balance between work and play. A friend who does much of his business on the golf course is very bright. He is also a powerful Irish maverick who sometimes drives his CEO nuts but he consistently brings in the highest revenues, is very popular in the company and rarely suffers from stress.

When I use this Irishman as an example, the response is often that he is a senior employee, it is easier for him to take the time to play golf. He would say that managing his work life this way is how he got to the top. He doesn't call it life balance but he agrees with me that when he is healthy and when he allows his clients to have that same feeling of well-being, he both gets the deals and sleeps well at night.

The secret of getting to the top and staying there comfortably is to figure out your own way of keeping balance. Of course, there is a lot more to balance than just keeping work and play in the level position on your mental scales.

Even the most balanced of us lose it from time to time. There is nowhere to hide from the stresses of modern-day living. A farmer I know well in Scotland, who appears to have the perfect life, his own land, environmental awards for his treasured woods, a good partnership with his wife, gets highly stressed from time to time and so does she. The demands on them are very high and they do not leave the farm often enough. When they do, it is just for the odd week of holiday. When they come back they fall into the old routine. The same pattern sets up again. So there goes the *if-only-I-lived-in-the-country* escape wish.

Balance is something you have to work on wherever you live and in whatever circumstances. There is no shortcut and once you have it established in your life you have to keep fine-tuning it. It is an on-going dance. You can't say, 'I have it now, it's fixed for life.' You need to know yourself so well that you, first establish the kind of balance you want, and, second, recognise the first signs of any tilting.

When you plan a holiday, you spend quite a long time researching where you want to go, looking at brochures, discussing it with your friends or family, checking on the travel company, the hotels, the benefits and prices of different airlines. You need to go through a similar process in planning your life. People think about their lives in commercial breaks between television programmes, when out jogging or during other fragmented pieces of time, but rarely do they schedule in time that is dedicated for the purpose.

Coming to work with me also forces my clients to put time aside for themselves. Some say they feel wicked, self-indulgent, others that it is the first time they have taken any structured time to plan their own needs. And since your life is likely to be longer than a holiday, why not put in a corresponding amount of time to get it the way you want it.

I told one client she would benefit from spending half an hour a day planning the balances and checks of her life – in her employer's time. She responded that she couldn't possibly, she was being paid to work all day. I suggested gently that if she took the time her company would benefit. We compromised at fifteen minutes. She would stop her phone, close the door of her office, sit quietly and think through what she needed to do and how she could stay in balance while achieving it. She still comes to me from time to time for some fine-tuning of her plans and last month I received a postcard from her from Beijing. 'If you hadn't told me to take the time to think through my strategy every day, I wouldn't be here. Thank you.'

The best way to start any plans you are trying to make is to think of all the things you need to do that aren't work. Put them into your time and your schedule first. Start to plan your time as if you don't have a career. How would you like it to be? If you don't want to work at all when you play around with this, then you have some serious decisions to make. I start one of my lectures on *Life Strategies* with a picture of a beach and a palm tree. I look at my audience and when they laugh and say, 'Yes please!' I ask, 'If that's what you want, why are you sitting here?'

Most people find they can't actually fill a whole week with non-work pursuits. Go on, slot them in, all the pleasures, all the sports items, the lectures, the outdoor life, meditation, yoga. What's left, what have you got to play with in terms of work? Two days, three, four and a half? If you were doing all these non-work pursuits, how much better would you feel? If you were doing half of them? None? Where is your well-being line?

Unless you get this well-being line clear you are making life very hard for yourself. If you constantly carry around a sense of being out of kilter, not calm enough, not strong enough, not well enough connected to your friends, you just aren't functioning properly. When you are like this you don't have enough to give to your career. When you don't give your career enough, you don't get enough sense of well-being from that either.

Career has to sit on top of a very solid sense of well-being. When someone asks how you are in the morning when you get to the office you have to mean it when you say you are fine. If you are not, then you are straining yourself all day. That is too hard on you. Nor are you giving your company good value.

Value-added is what we talk about when we are offering services to clients; it is also what we need to be bringing into our daily work lives. You cannot do this unless you are brimming with health and feeling emotionally and mentally alive (for more on this, see Chapter Six).

When you have this solid basis you can take more risk in your day-to-day life. So often I hear people say, 'I can't add anything else to my life, it is too full already.' That is exactly my point, you have to start thinking the other way around. The most important factor of your life is that you feel balanced and secure. Once you have that, you add as many work challenges as you can lay on top. As soon as you start to tip, or feel overwhelmed, you have to stop and check your balance line. Your balance line is the point at which you start feeling you are overworked or stressed. Get to know this fine line, be very aware of it.

To start thinking about how you balance the different parts of your life, do the exercise overleaf. Think about the different components of your life, write each in one of the boxes and put a percentage on it.

Imagine you are the figure at the top and put one of the current influences of your life in each of the boxes. Then put a percentage under each box. You may laugh at yourself. One of my clients filled the first two boxes with work and family and then stopped. He had already run out of his hundred per cent. This was George Bain, the one who had hired me to decided whether to take another term in one of the hottest academic seats in Europe or start a new phase of his life.

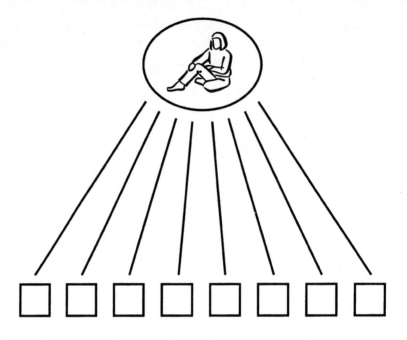

George had got to the point where almost everything he did was allied to work. So dinners out were work, lunches were with sponsors or course participants in the school. Work filtered into his weekends in the country. When he saw his boxes and realised that he couldn't get past the second, he started to think he might want to start a new phase in his life.

We worked together through this programme to set him a clear, balanced, forward-moving structure. Because of my association with the London Business School, giving lectures and being chair of the Media Group, one day, when I was there teaching, several lecturers came up to me and asked, 'Why did you take him away from us? He's been the best principal here in a long time.' 'I didn't take him away,' I answered, 'I just showed him that there were lots of other successes and joys. He chose to head for some of them.'

The next step for you to do is the same exercise but filling the boxes with the way you would like your life to run and then putting new percentages under these. This gives you a visual you can a work with. Keep it in mind in your day-to-day life. Don't let any of the boxes drop out. I find it startling sometimes the parts of their lives that people let drop out. And if your attention isn't on something important to you,

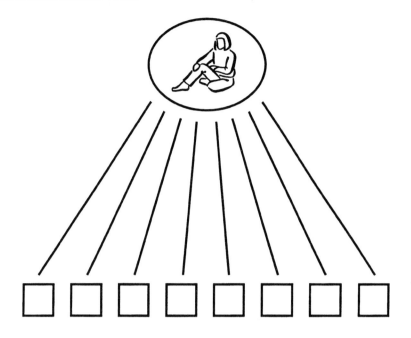

then you need to put it there. At this point you are looking for an indication of what you want. You may want to come back to this and check to see if you wish to add any boxes as you go through the programme.

Working with a woman who had her own business for twenty-five years and had just sold it, I had to deal with her scepticism about these boxes. 'I've succeeded on my intuition, I don't want to start putting my life in boxes now.' I explained to her that what I was asking for was far from trying to box her in; what we were trying to do was bring some neglected areas of her life up to the same level as her business. She is very strong willed and it is probably her will as much as anything else that made her success. She moaned and grumbled and didn't draw the second diagram.

When she came back two weeks later she was laughing, 'I can see what you mean now. By not drawing in the new balance I was just trying to stay with what I had done before. I think there was some of me that didn't believe I could actually have a new career, even though I had sold the business and wanted something new. Thank you. I feel much freer now, less boxed in!'

When I talk about working out the balance you want and suggest drawing diagrams it isn't that I want you to lose any spontaneity. Setting a framework within which to work your life allows more spontaneity. Awareness of your strengths and weaknesses allows you, just as you would with a business plan, to make the kind of research-based decisions that will give you the soundest approach given the product – that is you and your truths – that you have to work with.

TOOLS

- Draw your own version of the chart on the previous page, making sure that you are the one pulling the strings and that the boxes or circles or whatever you use sit at the same level.

- Think about how many components there are in your life, fill in the boxes with them and put a percentage on each one.

- Do the same chart again. This time add in the new elements you want to add to your life and do the percentages again.

CHAPTER TWO

BALANCING YOUR DREAMS

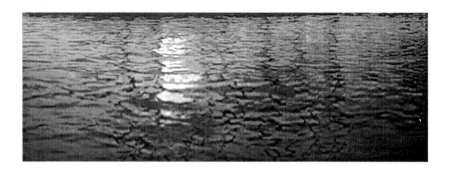

Here you look at your whole field of ideas, open up your most inspirational horizons and start to balance these with your more focused realities.

You take a more playful approach to your realities and a more serious approach to viewing the fullest extent of your inspirations. The gain is the clear, clean empty space in your mind, which will allow you to move beyond the frustrations of your everyday swirl.

You are sitting reading this book, perhaps dreaming a little, perhaps thinking, I know what I want to do if only circumstances would allow me. It is just that my family take too much time or I don't have the skills or there isn't that kind of work near where I want to live. You can go around and around in your head with these kind of thoughts, spend a lot of mental and emotional time, and when you don't move or act on them, you add frustration to the swirl.

I worked with an attractive thirty-something who ran her own business and who had taken a weekend personal development course. She had worked out a huge vision for herself but, three months later, still had very little idea on how to go about it. She was, she said to me, going to change the life of every woman in the UK. Could I help her?

She had, because of the collective pressure and hype of the weekend, gone beyond her usual common sense. The dream was too far from her and she was stuck between wanting it very badly and feeling not good enough because she hadn't been able to take any steps.

Your dreams are a good deal of what keeps you going, without them you are barely alive. Without a balance between these dreams and the reality of your life you are straining to be alive. There is a constant contradiction going on and you suffer. In my client's case, this inability to start working on her dream or vision was eating away at her self-confidence. She had, actually, become so unbalanced in this inner tug of war, that she had fallen down the stairs at her office. Her current business was beginning to be affected and she was also beginning to feel overwhelmed and anxious. 'How can I start my dream if I can't even manage my usual life?' she asked.

FINDING A CLEAR FOCUS IN YOUR FIELD OF IDEAS

In moving towards the new life balance you need to get as many of your ideas and thoughts out of your head as you can. Imagine, for a few moments, that you are sitting in a field with tall grass. Settle quietly and open your mind to ideas and possibilities for your life. As each one comes in, mentally throw it out to land on a blade of grass. See how many of these blades of grass you can attach an idea to. Get them all out into the open.

Sit with your ideas a while, observe each one with detachment. They are just ideas. At this point you do not mind whether you do

them or not. All you want is to find a place for them that isn't in your head. When you think you have finished, find at least twelve more, squeeze every last one out. Look around the field. Spread out for you is your field of ideas

While you are going through this programme and this balancing process, keep them there, at a distance, until I suggest you start working with them. Keep this airy, spread-out feeling, keep the distance between your day-to-day life and these ideas for a while. You will feel lighter and less cluttered.

YOUR MOST INSPIRATIONAL HORIZONS

At this stage look around the field and be pleased with yourself. This is your horizon, these are your possibilities. In this field of ideas are your aspirations, your hopes, your dreams and your needs. As a wind ripples across the field they move and bend and perhaps face a different way, perhaps even change form. Watching them move, you start to understand that your horizons are more flexible than you thought, that there are more possibilities than the fixed ideas in your mind. Letting your gaze wander through the grass, start to let your mind flow across the field in all directions; idly go beyond the ideas you have there and move towards whatever might be.

I remember when I worked at *Vogue* as the travel editor and sat in the features department, we used to think up titles together – the features editor, the copy writer, the features assistant, the literary editor and I. We would play around with ideas until they got crazier and crazier. Then, just as we were collapsing with laughter over our efforts, someone would come in with the good one. But it was the process of stretching our minds and getting beyond their usual horizons into the realms of foolishness that allowed us to find the inspiration we needed.

THE WHOLE FIELD

One of the reasons for doing this exercise is to realise just how many ideas you have already and to know that as you sit quietly you keep coming up with more. We worry that we will run out of ideas, dry up. We don't, ever, we just leave them there stagnant and can't get past them when we start to think. We all have too many ideas. Viewing them as a field is a good visual way of keeping them in their place.

By spreading them out in the field, each has a place at a distance from you, but none is more important, so you don't have to do anything with them. It's such a relief; they are all out there swaying in the breeze and you are here reading this with a clear head. For the moment, just leave them there, put them on hold; we will return to your field later in the programme.

REALITIES

Of course, while these ideas are out there, you can consider the realities of your life. Now that there is this wonderful clean, clear, empty space in your mind, which activities or ideas would you want to be engaging in passionately enough to clutter it up? If there is a perfect equilibrium in your mind without all that jumble you just separated and left in the field, which ideas are worth it to you to pursue and thereby risk getting out of that equilibrium?

I once sold a house before I had bought a new one. With my family, we moved into a rented flat and stored our belongings. I had collected 'things', some valuable, some just curious, from all around the world in my job as a travel editor, so much so that one of my dinner guests once said he couldn't find a place to put down his ashtray. At the end of the year, I sat my family down and asked them to make a list of what they really wanted from storage, with the suggestion that we would sell the rest. I limited myself to a dozen items and they decided to follow suit. Thirty-six items for three people. I called in the auctioneers and the rest disappeared.

After this clarifying exercise we needed less space, so instead of looking for another house, we were able to buy a beautiful, peaceful flat by the water, in Sydney, just ten minutes from the centre of town, the beach and the Opera House. Interestingly the items we had selected started to tell a new story for us. We started to get new ideas about the way we wanted to live. We choose a simpler, quieter look.

From this new base, we started to take up different interests; from the calm we were able to take more risks with our lives and take on new ventures. The fact that this process ultimately led to a divorce may put you off. But to me it was this clearing process that made me feel light enough to even consider such a risk. At the bottom of all the cover I had around me was the reality of my life, that it was time to make a serious change.

I have a client who had both his own company and was on the board of four other companies in the same field. He was so stuck in the realties of all this he couldn't even look out at the inspirational horizons. He had an ill-defined sense of wanting to change his life. He sold his own company before he came to me. But, what he had done was to fill his working days with the four board positions and talk to the same people he had talked to before. He couldn't understand why he still felt stressed, why he didn't feel more enthusiastic.

He started a new relationship and threw his energies intensely into that. At first this solved his gap; relationships are realities and he thought he understood realities. What he didn't understand, though, was that he still hadn't investigated what might lie on a further horizon for himself. He hadn't taken the time to find out what his dreams might be; he was firmly stuck in his realities.

Although he had lightened his load, he hadn't changed his way of thinking, expanded his ideas to include the ridiculous, the impossible and the inspirational. The relationship didn't work because he brought all of his old self to it – the ability to throw himself at something intensely and make it happen. He was so far out of balance in himself, and therefore in his relationship, that he knocked the woman over. She, overwhelmed, moved away; he felt rejected and the whole thing collapsed.

It makes sense to take a more playful approach to your realities and a more serious approach to letting more inspiration into your life. When you walk into the office in the morning, walk in with a skip and a smile. When you sit in your field of ideas, view very seriously the fullest extent of your inspirations.

TOOLS

- Sit quietly and imagine all your ideas spreading out over a field of tall grass, attaching each idea to one blade.

- When you think you have all your ideas spread out, think of another twelve.

- Close the picture and keep it stored in your mind until you come to Chapter Five.

CHAPTER THREE

BALANCE AMID THE TURBULENCE

I n times of turbulence there are two things you must do to get you freely and smoothly through. First, make a clear assessment of the changing situation you have come to. Second, take a clear view of the context in which you are sitting.

Approaching turbulence in this two-tier way means you solve the situation you are in before you even think of moving in a new direction. Your gain is that you fully understand where you are most powerful and where you can achieve the most.

This is a more strategic life-view, one that gives you time to step back from busy jobs, take stock, consider what you want out of life and decide whether you are heading in the right direction.

Turbulence, turbulence: as the world moves forward faster and faster around us, the signposts change so quickly that sometimes all we recognise is the turbulence. We are buffeted constantly. Our reponses are too often to try to go faster, to go harder or to retreat into our shell and focus on a smaller world. In the early 1970s there was a show with a popular song in it that struck people's souls – 'Stop the world, I want to get off'. Some did that, but the beat generation discovered that while you could be quite famous if you 'got off' in dope and dirgy poetry, you were quickly left behind. In the 1990s we know 'getting off' doesn't work; in fact, many are so frightened of being left behind and run so fast to keep up that they lose themselves in the rush.

I constantly see people in their forties and fifties who are convinced their lives are over, they are tired from too much turbulence. They are also so used to the turbulence they are quite frightened of the idea of not having it. Quite often I work with thirty-somethings from the financial institutions and they have fast-tracked through their careers to such an extent that they think life is over for them too. They have no other side or shades to their lives and can only imagine golf waiting ahead. Many feel so caught, so buffeted, so out of control of their lives that they do not know where they are.

RECOGNISE YOUR CHANGE POINTS

It used to be that we had promising early years, then a mid-life crisis, and twenty or so years later we retired. Because of longer life expectation, the changing structure of the business picture and our own increasing awareness and expectations, we now have many more *Change Points* to think about. Change Points are any times when you need to step back from busy jobs, take stock, consider what you want out of life and decide whether you are heading in the right direction.

Career Change Points come in early, mid and late career, in your thirties, forties, fifties and sixties. Other Change Points include successes and failures, illnesses, stress, moves overseas, redundancies and retirement. Major Change Points are when you try to change too many things at once.

Speaking at the Personal Development Fair in London in 1997, I was asked by a man in the audience how to handle change when too many things come at once. I asked him what sort of things and he started to list them. I cut him off at around point four; that's too many already. If you are being hit by so many Change Points at once, then tackle the easiest ones first, the ones you know how to do. Do not make a move until you are sure of having completed at least one of these points. Once you have made one happen the others start to fall into place. If it is your choice to try several Change Points at once, then think again, you are just making life difficult for yourself.

One of the most common strains I hear is, 'I'm really fed up with my job. If I can just hang on until Christmas/my holidays/the end of the financial year, I'll be OK.' Perhaps or perhaps not, but why not look at the Change Point now, solve it and move on?

In the first session when I work with clients I ask them what kind of a Change Point they have come to. The most important thing is to recognise that that's what it is and not be fazed by it. A female client in one of the international management consultancies, after seven years of fast-track, walked out of her job one day. She precipitated her own Change Point. She called me the next day and came to work with me very intensely, over a period of three weeks.

So keen was she to move on that she didn't take enough time to figure out why she had walked out. She was highly employable so she soon found a new international strategy job through a friend. I helped her through the change and helped her to negotiate the new contract. She wasn't interested, though, in spending more time to find the reasons she had come to the point of walking out, preferring to see it as a one-off event in her life.

Two weeks into the new job she walked out again. Walking out wasn't a pattern in her life but there was something else. She was a very competent, focused person, so used to achieving her goals that she couldn't see, and did not want to see, that there were underlying reasons for her frustrated explosion. Taking the same kind of job again, she repeated the behaviour – the frustration was still there. She had insisted it was to do with the way the company was run. What she hadn't stopped to do was to recognise what in her had triggered the Change Point.

She was a person who didn't like uncertainty. And when you come to a Change Point you get uncertainty; how can you not as you take one certainty apart and replace it with another? As you go through the steps, you have to make decisions, and to make a decision you have to

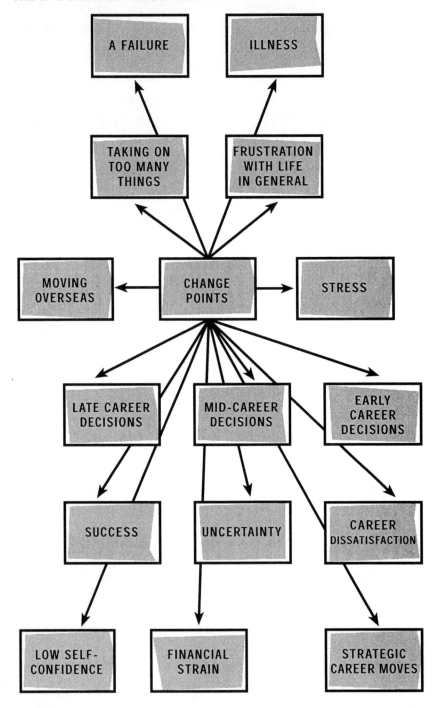

make up your mind. In making up your mind, your mind goes through stages when it doesn't have the right answers, so you get uncertainty, and uncertainty is uncomfortable.

A man who works in New York has the same behaviour but it manifests itself in his personal life, not his career. In business he is like a rock through difficult times. He ploughs through, tough, clear and determined. He recently started a relationship with a woman whom he was quite sure he was immediately and deeply in love with. This was what he had been waiting for all his life. Why hadn't he met her and married her, instead of his wife of fourteen years, from whom he was now divorced, he asked himself? Then he wouldn't have had to go through the living hell of his marriage, he thought.

These two had a marvellous time for six months, everything running smoothly. They agreed on everything, it seemed; they wanted the same things, it seemed; they had similar East Coast backgrounds. One fine day the whole affair came to a grinding halt. He suddenly became very uncertain. Was this the right woman? Did he want this any more? Was this the same woman he had met and loved so easily?

He hit uncertainty and he didn't like it. He ignored her for a few weeks. He rang one evening on his way home and went to see her, sitting there staring as if to get back his clarity, one way or the other. He was so uncomfortable in this state of uncertainty that he decided to back off. He split away from the uncertainty, broke off the relationship and went back to being safely certain on his own. 'Odd,' he told a friend, 'there was so much, and now I feel nothing.' He wasn't actually feeling nothing, but by going back to a familiar state, certainty, he was able to bury the uncomfortable uncertain feelings.

A friend from San Francisco, Janie Ligon, who was running Levi Strauss in the UK until recently, handles this uncertainty better. Over lunch one Sunday she was talking about trying to decide whether to stay for three years longer in the UK or go back to a new job at headquarters in San Francisco. She is one of the most decisive women I know; apart from her niceness, honesty and intelligence, this is how she got to be chief executive.

In the four weeks when both she and the company were trying to work out whether the job available was the right one for her at this point, she was feeling horrible. 'I hate this, there are too many pieces, too many changeables. I keep wondering, for instance, is this the right path upwards? Would it be selfish to leave my daughter behind in England to finish school? Am I right to leave Europe after only three years? If I stay here, will another slot come up when I want it?' She grinned wryly, 'But that's the way these times are, insecure, and I'll live with it.'

One of the least considered Change Points is an illness. If you have become ill, whether with cancer, flu or a strained back, if the body is under-performing in some way, then you have reached a Change Point. People with Aids, for an extreme example, have to undergo a major life-change to live longer physically and to cope with the psychological effects of the disease. But for anyone, any malfunctioning in the body is a message that you have to change something about the way your body is functioning and probably about the way you run your life.

Any Change Point involves a lot of decisions. The danger is that the thinking is left too late. This often happens when the first major Change Point comes up in the thirties. Until then the twenty-some-things are trying to fit in as much as they can, trying to investigate as many opportunities as possible. Planning a move in the right direction feels like a straitjacket, too strategic a way to behave, behaviour for the olds, who are seen as anything over early thirties. Twenty-somethings prefer the see-saws and swings of life, and why not? If they haven't set in some adventurous spirit at this point when are they going to learn it? Too often people wait until they retire to fit in those longed-for travels, adventures and new hobbies. I would rather see more of this adventurous behaviour from twenty-somethings, so that the concept can be explored, learnt and kept.

At any age frustration often turns into a Change Point. Initially it doesn't look like one but as it builds up it often blocks out any kind of future perspective. I notice from my practice that it is an undefined frustration and dissatisfaction with *LIFE* that often compels people to talk to me. Often someone will come in and say, 'I want to change my job, everyone treats me badly' or 'I have to move, there are no oppor-tunities there for me' or 'I want to do something more worthwhile, investment banking is too greedy'. If the reasons are quite general and unexplored, it is just frustration.

UNDERSTAND YOUR CONTEXT

Before any changes or planning are started I look at clients' histories and at their today, where they are themselves. Dissatisfaction with others is always a dissatisfaction with ourselves, but we tend to blame someone else for what we are experiencing. A very bright young woman in her thirties, working on the gilt markets, came to me, bounced into my sofa and announced she was going to leave her bank because no one cared about anything but making money. In the middle of the second session as we were sifting through some of her unachieved ideas (see Chapter Seven) she suddenly announced, 'I'm going to get a job in a charity or start a data base for charities.'

I often hear this kind of disenchantment with what are perceived as inflexible institutions. And I often hear the longing to do something that makes a difference. I once asked Peter Jennings, one of the three top-rating TV anchormen in the USA, why he had never gone back to law school, as he had had a yen to do for ten years or so. He answered, 'Because I can make more of a difference in this job than anywhere else.' Surprising you might think. Peter is a screen personality and an intelligent commentator, but, make a difference? 'I care about the situations I deal with and if I can go on giving as much of a balanced point of view as is possible in my kind of show, I'm making a difference.'

Peter stops one night after we have dinner to talk to a man begging on the street. He is concerned that the beggar should know there is a refuge for him and makes sure he understands exactly where it is. Peter understands power, knows how to use it well, and he can make more of a difference on television using that power than he would serving at the refuge. He knows what his context is.

My bright young woman hears of an opportunity to start a charitable business with a man who believes he has a new cause for which to raise money. What she finds, as we look into this opportunity, is that there are a great many good causes out there and not enough money to go around. What about looking where the bank spends its charitable money, I asked her, could she have some input or influence there? Could she act as a matchmaker for her bank and a cause she would like to further. She is sitting in a place where there is money. Why not use her skills to direct some of it or some more of it towards where it is most needed.

At the same time she can keep her large salary and probably influence more money in one charitable transaction than a new charity is going to find in its first two years. It isn't that I discourage my clients from starting their own business, but it is important to understand where you are most powerful, in what context you can achieve the most.

What has happened to this young woman is that, by realising it is herself she needs to understand better and by not reacting against the attitudes of the people around her, she changes her own attitude. She is through her Change Point intact, and she has added to her life, in her own context, not run away from it. I always ask clients to solve their situations first, to understand the context around them, before they move in a new direction. If they don't they will just repeat the Change Point again, probably again and again, until they run away or it gets so bad they are forced to change in unfavourable circumstances.

CHAPTER FOUR

BALANCING YOUR
ENVIRONMENT

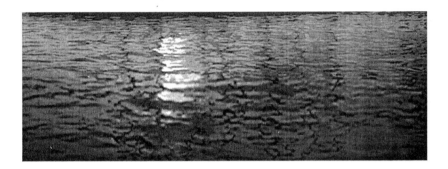

T he most essential decisions you have to make to have a more balanced life are the ones that set up your environment in the most
effective way. Making these decisions often involves changing
your perceptions on what you, your family and your organisations want.

Achieving a balanced environment in our exponentially changing
world requires continuous creativity, innovation and the leveraging of
your resources. What you have always to keep in the forefront of your
thinking is that at any point of your life you stand in the middle of your
environment with an essential tool-kit of your own resources. There are
always crucial decisions to be made, and in our time these have to be
continuously rethought.

To have what you need from your company or organisation you may
have to educate them to respond to the growing demand for individuality in employment. In the new, more transparent, flatter business environment you can be in a very strong position to create a mutually useful
ongoing alliance with your organisation. The more you achieve this, the

better the position you will be in to shape a role for yourself.

What do you think your environment is? How flexible do you think it is? When you think of your environment do you have the sense that everything around you is supportive and brings good towards you? Or do you feel your environment is unclear, your life cluttered, your thoughts a little untidy and you have too many things in one area of your environment and not enough in another?

MAKING YOUR ENVIRONMENT WORK FOR YOU

I am constantly amazed at how little people allow themselves to do in their lives. We blame society, our companies, our families, – *'If it wasn't for so and so or this situation I would do it'*. What our families and companies want for us is to be well-rounded, fulfilled, fully operative people. We are so conditioned to feeling guilty if we don't do what others want us to do that we use it as an excuse not to do whatever it is we're not doing. We blame our environment in one way or another, without seeing that it is our essential responsibility to see that we make our environment work for us.

I had a call recently from a woman who had worked with me on her *Life Strategy* and was just about to sign a contract for a new job. 'I need to come and see you first,' she said, 'you have such a good way of fitting in all the pieces I want to make fit.' We are conditioned to think that we have to sacrifice, give up ourselves, when we make career choices. I'm not keen on the notion of sacrifice; to me it means we have let a piece of ourselves be killed off. If we think of our environment as a wonderfully mysterious, ongoing puzzle we can build in anything we want.

There is a far too powerful myth that we all work full-time and that is what our companies expect us to do. In the UK, for example, forty-four per cent of the population is not in full-time work and this percentage is rising. We see the tide of people rushing to work in the morning, their cars bumper to bumper, the buses full, and because this tide looks physically like so many of us we believe this is what we are all doing. To add to the picture, because companies and institutions are the meat of large sections of both the editorial and the advertising of our newspapers, we daily receive more information about them than we do about what the other forty-four per cent are doing.

As individuals we think we are outnumbered and outpowered by these companies and institutions. We know that their bargaining power in the market is huge. And, because we want the safety that we credit them with because of their power, we want a position in that safety.

The real picture is quite different to the perceived myth. In reality the shape of all our personal environments as well as the bigger environment we live and work in is changing so exponentially that the corporate or institutional environment is no longer the safest place, neither is its future behaviour predictable.

Talking to one of the American Fortune 500 companies, one that is considered to have a good loyalty culture, I was appalled at their short-term, narrow-view, fluctuation approach to company versus employee well-being when the bottom line is threatened. The human resources director said to me quite matter of factly, as if there would obviously be no discussion, 'We have great employee benefits in the good times, and we hire on that; but now we are downsizing and closing plants, laying off a lot of people, these benefits have to go for the employees we do keep.'

The most important point you have to remember in this constantly changing and sometimes too reactive business environment is that there are always new solutions to look for, the new always happens. If you keep looking for these, as creatively as you know how, you are an integral part of the changes that are happening, not a victim of them. You may need to change your perceptions on what you, your family and your organisation want.

TAKING ADVANTAGE OF A CHANGING ENVIRONMENT

Let's look at the changing picture for a moment. What are the changes in our environment at this point? If you look at the illustration overleaf you can see very clearly some of the current elements we are dealing with. You may want to add some of your own.

In this shifting picture we are constantly having to weigh up such issues as innovation versus operational efficiency, short-term success versus long-term planning, a bigger reach in society versus more isolation, the advancing formalised knowledge base of technology versus the importance of ambiguity and the eccentric.

Achieving a balanced environment for yourself in this exponentially changing world requires most of all a constant creativity, innovation and the continuous leveraging of your resources. There has never been a time when innovation and continuous creativity have been so central. Because technology is changing the size and shape of our environment so fast, as well as the way we function on a day-to-day basis, we need to hold open the shape of that environment.

We know that in fifteen years we will be able to attach ourselves to a computer and gain a hundred million times our brain power. Taking the open environment concept a little further into the realms of possibilities, in the year 2200, future research shows we may well develop into a biological/technical/emotional organism that moves from planet to planet, picking up a body form to use where and when we need it.

Coming back to the planet again, it is not the environment you work in but the way you work in any environment that counts. The people who know how to build good alliances with their companies, whether internally or externally, for example, are the ones who succeed whether they work from home or in the company environment. We are being required to be more and more individual, to take more and more responsibility for how we set up our own environment, to be personally, as well as organisationally, continuously creative and innovative.

NEW MILLENNIUM FOCUS ON UNKNOWN CHALLENGES

TECHNOLOGY/ QUANTUM PHYSICS

SOCIETY BIGGER REACH, MORE ISOLATION

ENVIRONMENT DISTINCTION BETWEEN FULL & PART-TIME WORK BLURRING

INDIVIDUAL GLOBAL

LONGER LIFE 3 CAREERS MULTI-CHANNEL LIVES

COMPETITION/ TURBULENCE

SHORT-TERM SUCCESS LONG-TERM PLANNING

CONTINUOUS CREATIVITY & BOTTOM LINE EFFICIENCY

I worked with the managing director of an international company, initially to sort out how to balance his home and office life during the period when his wife was dying. Should he give up his job? Should he become non-executive? Would it be better to be at home with his wife? She wanted him to go on working because she felt he would need to when she was gone. We thrashed all this out, changing his schedule so that he had some more time with her, but making it work so that when she was gone he had positioned himself for moving on to the chairman role, still with the more limited hours.

In working out a more flexible schedule for him we started to talk about the senior executives in his company, an issue that had been worrying him. 'They are travelling a good deal and are having trouble relating to their home world.' I recommended a new programme for these people, which would give them three-day weekends once a month, clearly scheduled and marked for everyone they are working with to know about and be prepared for. Doing it this way, I suggested, would be a continuing release on the pressure valve, both for the individual, their families and the company.

I am quite sure that not one of those executives would have come to their boss to ask for this kind of time off, figuring that the company was locked into the usual structure. It is there for you; most human resources people are happy to talk, it's just that they are not yet aware of nor trained to think up these kinds of environmental possibilities.

One of the subjects I have just started to give talks on is how organisations need to respond to the growing demand for individuality in employment. As an individual you may have to educate your company to this way of thinking.

At a time when we know we are looking at more short-term careers with our companies, we have to be more flexible ourselves. I hear too many people being frightened of this change; the best approach you can take is to be ahead of it.

If you think that flexibility is going to be one of the most useful qualities in your working life, you are going to be safer in the current climate. If you think of your company as your ally, as an entity with which you will build strategic alliances in the same way you build a strategic alliance with a supplier or service provider, you shift the balance away from the traditional employer/employee agreement.

With a more transparent business climate we have also become more aware of our companies' needs. The more you know about these needs the more successful you are going to be. It is not enough to work out your own career strategy within the company as you see it now or over the next year. You need to look at the company's strategy for the next five years, ten if there is one, and if there isn't then find out what the strategic intent is for the next ten years.

To help you do this, find yourself three mentors in your company. These should be people who want your success and who see a future for you in the company's future. They would be above you in the company, preferably in different areas, with one at board or director level. It is useful if one is in the strategy area, one is on the financial side and another in general management.

Talk with these people on a regular basis, keep in touch with what the company is planning and how it is changing. If you do this you are in a better position to plan your own strategy as well as be more flexible. You are also less likely to get caught out if there are redundancies coming up. You need to look at this every month, keep fine-tuning your own position. If there are any major changes coming up, you will be in a position to shape a role for yourself.

Standing back, working hard and getting the job done are not enough either. In this fast-changing climate you need to keep re-inventing your own role. Apart from the obvious safety of this tactic, you will keep your work more interesting and give the employers the idea that you are an integral part of their strategy.

If you are already at board level, mentors are obviously in shorter supply, although the chairperson should be one of them. The other two can come from bench-marking relationships with people you admire in other similar companies. Maintain these relationships constantly and carefully, too. At this level the relationships work best if the traffic is two way; in fact, the best way to start them is to offer some of your knowledge to the person with whom you want to establish this mutual mentorship.

The next step is to invent two or three roles for yourself, making sure they are in line with the company's strategy by checking and discussing them with your mentors. The more pro-active you are the better position you are in to negotiate with your company to get the environment you want.

Make sure your company understands that you are developing an alliance with them in your plan – that you do not want something just for yourself, but that you have seen a niche or a possibility in their strategy that together you can develop or fill. You are looking for something that will make both parties stronger, that gives each an equal amount of benefit. In these alliances you are looking to progress your relationship with the company and theirs with you. You make of your alliance something that is more living, more malleable.

When you do this it is harder for them to think of letting you go if they hit hard times. You start to develop a more progressive mindset and this is a value added. You take a lot of stress out of your life because you have built a secure position, balanced between your and your company's ongoing needs. Because you have put time into devel- oping this, there is more of your individuality involved.

In today's flatter companies it is easier to take our place in the environment because the environment is so much more plastic. Take the Microsoft environment, for example, one that is based on exponential creativity and success. Everything is geared to that, including the soft drink machines and canteens, which enable the twenty- and early-thirty-something employees to keep working without leaving what is known as the campus. While I was waiting at reception one day I heard a young man on reception say to a friend on the phone, 'You ll have to suggest where we meet, I almost never leave here.'

In an open green-lawn-surrounded series of low-rise buildings, fountains and outdoor chairs and umbrellas are dotted around. The actual offices are virtually trenches. Each person has practically his or her whole life in there – they look like teenagers' rooms; each employee has brought in enough personal stuff to help him or her survive the long hours required to get and keep the jobs in the top development groups, the jobs with the highest stock options. There are often seven or eight computer screens and the assorted technology to go with them.

But these people know the company places a high value on them as individuals even if it works them like crazy for the four or five years most of them stay. Amongst these there is one young man who works half-time. The general view is that he gets away with it because he is so extraordinarily talented. The real story is that he likes a more var-ied environment, so he educated Microsoft into believing that he is indispensable. This young man actually can't be different enough to be the only one in the top development groups to have this much lee-way; the whole of Microsoft doesn't depend on this one person's brain power. But he is so good at educating his company to want for him what he wants, that he has carved himself out a unique position.

What you always have to keep to the front of your thinking is that at any point of your life you stand in the middle of your own environment with an essential tool-kit of your own resources. There are always crucial decisions to be made and these have to be continuously rethought.

I had a conversation recently with a friend who had just been to his thirty-year reunion at Harvard. He had brought the Harvard classroom to a standstill one day, during a case-history session that was based on the class members, thirty years on. When this case history came to key values, he plunged in and went a little deeper than either he, or those around him, had expected. He sailed into his emotions and, in doing so, allowed the others' success stories in the room to sail into theirs.

He had built himself a very successful environment; a man with a PhD in engineering, a second arts degree and an MBA from Harvard, he has, step by step, over his life, developed for himself the kind of per-sonal and work environment many would envy. His life includes a healthy variety of achievements – including a period at McKinsey, being treasurer for a political party, managing director of a major arts organi-sation and, for the last ten years, working as a quietly power-ful strategic consultant to blue chip international clients. As he moved from his forties to his fifties he also built in more time to pursue his own interests and spend big sections of time with his wife and children shar-ing their interests, including camel riding across the desert with his son.

At this Harvard reunion he startled everyone by talking about two crystallising situations in his life, his near divorce and his cancer. He told them that when he had come to these two places he had had to make some core decisions about what was important to him about being alive. He recounted a conversation he had had with his wife, while in hospital, after his cancer operation. His wife said to him that if he wanted to keep working he should at least give up chairing the fund-raising drive he had undertaken for his daughter's school and concentrate on looking after himself while he went through the chemotherapy. She put up a good case and he agreed with her.

When he woke up the next morning, though, he realised something very different about his attitude to living. Yes, he would expand the time he spent at their weekend house and devote more time to one of his passions – the garden they were building there – and he would take on less work. But, if he might only have a year or a short time to live he wanted to spend that year contributing to the world he lives in. Sitting in the core of his life, contributing to the world around him, to his environment, was the way he wanted to go out of this world.

He did just that, and in a year he had raised the funds for the school. Five years later, here he was, going to his Harvard reunion, still working internationally some of the time, spending treasured days in art galleries and at the opera overseas, with the cancer totally in remission.

To achieve this he had to stand in the middle of his life, face his fears and understand the core value he wanted to place in the middle of his environment, contributing to the world he lives in. He fully believes this deep-level changing of his perceptions about what was important to him, that this kind of commitment to his environment – as well as taking good care of himself – has been the major contributor to his getting well again. His discussions with his family and his re-negotiations both with them and with his own life's structure had helped him to become closer to the essentials of his environment.

TOOLS

- List three changes happening in your environment.
- List five good, supportive elements in your environment.
- List three essential decisions you need to make to improve your environment.
- Look for three mentors and open discussions with them.

CHAPTER FIVE

BALANCING THE FUTURE

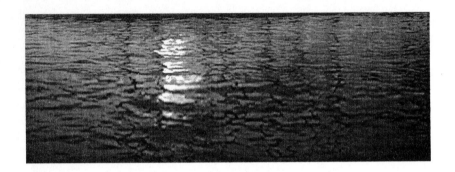

H ere are the mechanics you need to start building a balanced
future. Setting up the right structure, with clear directions for
planning your next step ahead, brings ease and a strong sense
of well-being.

The strongest way to build a balanced future is to look as far into the
future as you can and at the same time view the broadest spectrum. In
this way you can the belief that you can build as rich and varied a life as
you wish to.

To be solid in your future you need to stay close to the truth in your
life. By doing this, it is simpler for you to live in, to explain, to move with
and stay in balance with the truth of your life.

YOUR BROADEST SPECTRUM, YOUR LONGEST VIEW

The strongest way to build a balanced future is to open up your view as much as you can. At this point you need to look both at the broadest spectrum of you life and at the longest-term view you can possibly imagine. When people's lives fall out of balance, what they very often do is to bunker down, pull in, retreat, saying, 'If I just focus on what I'm doing, everything will fall into place.'

To start thinking about this broad spectrum, go back to your field of ideas for a moment (see page 27). Look at all these unconnected ideas waving there in the wind. Imagine that in your life you have time to do every one of these ideas, that they are the panorama of your possibilities. Spread them out in a new panoramic, broad spectrum form. Each and every one of them is a part of you and each and every one of them is something you would like to have in your life. If you neglect them or leave them out of your life, you are missing out on something in you that wants to happen. They are the richness in you, the variety that makes you the individual that you are.

And, of course, you do have time to do each and every one of these ideas, if you structure them over the course of your lifetime. What happens too often is that these ideas keep getting left at the roadside in honour of the mainstream of your life, leaving you with a dissatisfied feeling that you are missing out on something. Just think for a moment. If you have forty years more to follow ideas, or thirty years more, or fifty, or just ten, couldn't you slot in all of them? Or most of them?

Have some fun for a few minutes and look at how this might work. Draw up a calendar that covers your longest view and see where you might want to put all these dreams. When I ask clients to do this they are usually surprised at how this looks because when they start slotting their dreams and ideas into a long time-frame like this they almost don't have enough ideas.

From this perspective, the long-term view starts to open up. When I worked with George Bain on this, he balked at looking down thirty years because we were actually trying to decide what his plans were for the next three years or so. We agreed on twenty years, and as he started to look at his options down that length of time, he realised he had room in his life for much more than he had thought. At first he started to wonder if he had enough; even twenty years is an awesome amount of time, if you haven't considered it before.

If you have difficulty doing this exercise, start by listing the myriad of things you have done in the same time period in your past. You will never get them all down; there are far too many to remember or catalogue unless you have kept a diary. But just the fact that your list gets totally unmanageable and too long will give you an indication of how much you can fit into your future.

If you keep the broadest spectrum of your life open, you always keep reaching for every piece of your nature and every possibility in you. It allows you to keep yourself open, ready for the new, receptive to unexpected opportunities.

At the same time, by looking as far down into the future as you can, you will hold the belief inherently that you can build as rich and varied a life as you wish to. You carry the belief that there is time to do everything you want to do. This runs counter to the way people usually think that they have to rush to get the basics of their lives fitted in, focus only on the most important, and that they will never have time to do all the things they want. Be logical for a minute. We live around seventy-five years on average; isn't seventy-five years long enough to carry out all those dreams?

By constantly reverting to the broadest spectrum and the longest view, you provide a marvellously unlimiting and balanced future framework for yourself within which to operate. It is when we shrink into the small that we become less effective. By keeping this unlimiting framework in mind you are saying that you step outside and beyond the narrows of life, that you are carving out a big space for yourself, your ideas and your possibilities.

BUILDING A FUTURE WHEN EVERYONE WANTS A PIECE OF YOUR TODAY

The most challenging part about building a new future is that the people around you still expect you to be the same old you and they still expect the same contact, connections and output from you. Futures are so easy to think about while you are on holiday, for instance, because you are outside these day-to-day entanglements and commitments.

Still, a future on your own wouldn't be much fun and if you ran away from everyone around you, you would just collect a new set of everyones around you in the new environment. So you've got them, these surrounding entanglements and commitments, and it's your job to manage them. They aren't an excuse. Blame will never get you the future you want; blame will probably get you a retreat from the future you want.

The first step is to be resoundingly clear about what your new future is. Could you say it in one sentence and then fly that one sentence on a flag above your house? Is it that clear, both to you and the people around you? If it isn't that clear to you, how can you expect those around you to respond well? If you have your future held into your heart, how can you expect others to understand and contribute?

If you don't have a future mapped out – *'I'll know it when I see it'* – then you really are making life difficult and confusing for the people around you. *'Where is she now?'* they will wonder. They won't have anything to attach to. Some people resist mapping out a future because they think it will inhibit them, but what it actually means is that you are still heading towards the future, but oscillating and remaining uncontactable.

One of my younger clients was trying to change jobs but every time she set up an interview or tried to find the time to write letters, her current job got in the way. 'I can't do this,' she wailed. 'There isn't any time for me.' She had allowed the people she works with to take over, to cross the boundaries into her territory.

It wasn't just a new job she didn't have the time to find, but time for herself to plan her day, her week, her month and her year. She has become entangled in the work situation rather than bringing the best of herself to the current circumstances. In this position she couldn't even build a better place for herself in the company; what they would be reading from her was reactive pack behaviour rather than individual contribution.

The most important way to build the future you want is to stand up and be counted on what you believe and where you are going. It isn't always easy for people to speak with clarity, but when you have clarity there isn't much argument. I always know, when I am speaking publicly for instance, when I have got it exactly right. There is a quiet in the room, a quiet that is there because people have recognised a truth that has been said.

At the funeral service for Diana, Princess of Wales, in 1997, there was an extraordinary moment when applause broke out amongst the people outside the cathedral watching a large television screen and then amongst the congregation inside. It happened because her brother, Earl Spencer, had spoken his truth, the truth as he saw it in regard to his sister's life. The fact that he had also spoken a universal truth helped, too: the truth that people around us do hound us and that we need enormous courage to stand as sure, as Elton John's vocal tribute put it, as a candle blowing in the wind.

The courage we need to build a future is very strengthening when we use it, and very weakening when we don't. It is much easier to take the norm than it is to go where our hearts want. It is easier to roll over and be hurt in the heart than it is to reach out for the adventurous and the new. We know hurt, we know what it feels like and we can deal with it. But we don't know what the other side, the new territory is going to feel like, so we hold back in what we think is a safe place. But this safe place isn't safe at all; retreating into it wears down our natural, spontaneous energy over and over again.

It is always interesting to me to hear people's admiration for inspirational sports people or actresses. What they do not see is that it is a bit of themselves they want in that sports star or actress whom they admire, a bit of themselves that is there but they don't let it out. So they crave for this state of brilliance or ecstasy through someone else. And instead of satisfying their own craving, they fill it with the craving of junk food or smoking, hardly wondering why it doesn't satisfy as the years rush by.

To be solid in your new future you need to eat bravery and courage for breakfast, lunch and dinner. When you do this the respect you will garner from everyone around you will give you more bravery and courage. It is self-feeding and it is centrally feeding. People are drawn to courage. They expect a smaller part of your today if you are following a passion or doing something that has a worth or a value to the society you live in. It was easier for Ghandi, for instance, to move his followers than it is for someone running a huge international financial institution. But, whatever the situation you are operating in, the closer you stay to where the truth is, the more effective you will be. The clearer you are about being close to the truth, the less resistance you get from those around you. The piquant point about being close to the truth in your life is that it is simpler for you to live in, to explain, to move and stay in balance with that truth.

TOOLS

- List every achievement you can think of since you started working, both in your private and personal life. This will quickly make you aware of how many achievements you can expect to make in the same period of your future.

- Draw up a calendar of the next ten, twenty or thirty years and put in all your dreams from Chapter Two.

- List all the areas of your life that would improve if you brought in bravery and courage.

- Write down the strongest truth you have and ask yourself if you have it placed centrally in your life.

PICTURES FOR A FUTURE

'If I only had a blank page to write my future on' people say. So I give them one, several in fact. There is an exercise you can do now that will help you build your new future. Use only your intuition to do it.

You need four pages of blank paper. Draw four picture frames, one on each. Doing this exercise will help you change the life-print you did in Chapter One. With these four forward-looking pictures you are setting in growing, changing and forward-moving life-prints.

Draw in each of the frames overleaf a picture of what you want in your life and how you want it to look (people, objects and places):

In the next six months:

In five years:

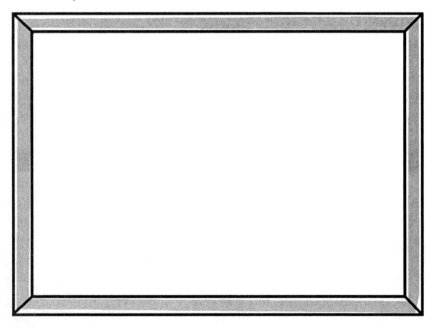

In ten years:

In twenty years:

This exercise to frame the future is useful because:

- Once you have drawn in what you want, you have a visual in your head that is harder to ignore than mere plans. Keep these visuals close to you so that they are a reminder of what is important to you in your future.
- You have to be selective because there is only so much that will go in one picture.
- You can see clearly how many new things you can fit in the four pictures over the twenty years.
- By doing this intuitively, you cut out all the extra stuff, the dead wood, the obligations that are out of date.

PLANNING A MOVE IN THE RIGHT DIRECTION

To plan a move in the right direction, you need to stand back, take stock and be as dispassionate as you know how. Be an observer in your life, move back, watch yourself doing what you do and how you do it. For a week, notice quietly everything you do. You may laugh a lot when you do this, you may sometimes want to cry.

This week of observation can be either when you are working or when you are on holiday, the important factor is to watch yourself quietly, so that you take a less involved position. One of the chief factors in stopping us from moving towards something we want fiercely is that we are too passionate about it, too involved in the outcome, and we lose the outsider's view.

It is important to maintain this outsider's view all the way through planning a new move. Staying outside allows you to be tidier about the decisions you need to make and clearer in staying with the plan you have set, and it keeps you from getting confused when distracting situations come into play. Staying outside allows you to see more quickly where and when you might start to fall out of balance. It is always easier for our friends or our family to see when we are out of balance, but the trouble with relying on them to tell us is that they see our situation from where they are sitting, not from our perspective.

Having established yourself as the amused observer in your life, it's time to get on with the planning. As the amused observer you can more easily do the research you need to do. I send my clients off to do a lot of research. For example, someone comes to me and says they want to move to France or Mexico or the rainforests of Australia. I ask them to allot a budget for the research, exactly as they would in their businesses, establish a time-frame and find out who are the people they need to see to make a decision. Find the answers to all the questions you cannot work out sitting on your sofa. If it doesn't look good at close quarters then you can chop this possibility out of your planning. If it does look good, then you have done the groundwork you will need to do when the time comes to move.

Planning is building a life for something you want to do, building the idea into an entity that has its own substance. You just keep building and building your plans until the point comes when they easily turn into a reality. You build your plans until they almost start on their own.

If a client has come up with a career decision, I ask them to look at a broad range of companies in the field, research them with due diligence, on the Internet, through contacts, by talking to people in the companies, by doing small things like taking lunch times in the vicinity of these companies.

For example, in the UK, there is a perception that if you work for a company such as entrepreneur Richard Branson's Virgin, there will not be any of the boring, heavier business ethics that you may often find stifling in your own companies. Research this before you apply, because although working for Branson may be exciting, it may just be too much of living in the new and on the edge to handle, given your background. The numbers may look good, the profile may be enticing and yet the day-to-day life within the business may not be running in a structured enough way.

It may, of course, suit you, and if all the signals are right, then you have done your research and are in a much better position to invent a role for yourself in the company. You will be able to go in and offer them something you have thought of, and that is a position of strength. In this kind of position you will be able to sit in your own balance when you do start and not get pushed and pulled by the unfamiliarity of the demands around you. If you decide not to go for a particular company, you are better informed about the market around the company you do choose.

TOOLS

- Establish yourself as the amused observer in your life.

- Research until you are bored; at this point you know enough.

- Build and build on your idea until it has a life of its own. When it gets to that stage it is time to start.

- Know that the best plans do have a life of their own, that they need to happen whether or not you do them. People are often afraid to share their plans for fear that someone else will steal them and do the same thing, but this very rarely happens.

- Make sure that your plan is original enough not to conflict with someone else's plan.

- If someone else if starting the same plan, either abandon yours or join forces.

- Once you have it all worked out, share you plan with at least five or six people before you decide to go ahead.

PART TWO

SORTING OUT YOUR PAST AND LOOKING AT YOUR FUTURE

In the second part of the programme you sort out the key life-influences that you have to work with. Balance these past and current influences in your life – work, family, friends, interests, health, mind – and you will have a clearer tomorrow. Here you change your perceptions about what you want to keep for the future and what you want to discard.

By reassessing your power and your inherent drivers you can more easily find the safety of a challenging future. By drawing on your success habits, you learn how to find the natural energy you need to attract the most interesting career moves and the most influential people.

CHAPTER SIX

BALANCING INFLUENCES

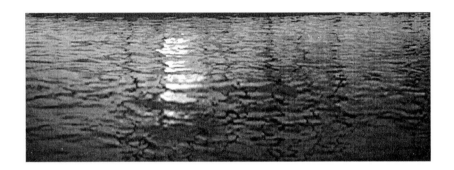

Make yourself aware of the influences in your life – the influences you carry around that drive your today and tomorrow. Balancing influences is a sensible, cleansing process to go through every year. You carry around so much in your mind and body that you hardly know what affect this has on you. Sorting these out will change your perceptions about what you want to keep in your life and what you want to banish.

These key influences – your body, health, mind, heart, spirit, emotions, power, relationships – are the base-line of you; they are your life-history. These vital players in your life, though, cannot be set in an appropriate balance until you add the totally new, something shiningly new you want to do, which, when you think of it, adds a sparkle to your eyes. Take the time to work carefully through these and your spirits will lighten.

Balancing your influences is a sensible, healthy process to go through thoroughly every year. You carry around many influences handed down from parents, fights with siblings, past careers, interests tried, loves abandoned, health patterns, adult relationships, childhood friendships, emotional history, brain habits and many more. You assume, since these influences are stored in your body and your mind, that you know all about them and they are just a base-line part of you.

They are a base-line part of you; they are your life-history. If you could print them out, you would have every clue you need to solve your own mystery. But as with everything else in your fast-moving world, your perception of them is constantly shifting and changing just as you shift and change.

Your perception is coloured by events. An emotion that has been sitting around for a long time may be such a familiar influence that it may act as a filter on your life. A familiarity with the emotion of loneliness, for example, may stop you from reaching out to ask someone to do something for you. The influence of being lonely may make you believe that is all you deserve so you stay in that emotion. It doesn't feel good but you come to fear that it feels better than being rebuffed.

These vital life-influences are the material you already have to work with. Understand them fully, root around in them for a couple of weeks. Be you own investigator. This chapter helps you assess the importance of each influence in your own situation and prompts you to re-value some. Be ready to smile when some old favourites come into focus. Learn to balance your life-influences and the turbulence will not hit you so hard.

THE HEALTH INFLUENCE

Here's the big one. Unless you have resoundingly good health, none of the rest is going to work. Health is the key influence on your life. Your body affects everything you do. I am constantly amazed at how people shrug off ill-health, live with headaches, sore places. Our bodies are the one tangible we know we have until the day we die. They are the vehicle we live in. I know quite a few people who take better care of their suits and shoes than their bodies.

A friend who has an irritated gall bladder said to me today, 'I haven't time to think about it now, I must finish writing my book.' When

I called her in on this, she answered, 'It's not so bad, I have only felt exhausted for a few days over the last two months. I must get on.' I wondered just how many days would be acceptable to her. When I suggested a two-week cleansing regime, she answered, 'Oh, I couldn't, what about going out to dinner? It would be too inconvenient for my hosts and people would think I was making a fuss.'

Making a fuss, about her health? She couldn't understand why her writing was going so slowly. She's my friend, not my client, so I couldn't push her as hard on just what number on her priority list she places her health. Certainly not high enough if it comes after her friends. But I did suggest a visit to a doctor and a reflexologist. Also that she walk more and take up some kind of stretching exercise. She rang me yesterday and told me that since she had done these simple things, she had also subsequently written a very fast 30,000 words.

You have to decide just what level of health is acceptable to you, what kind of health you want, and what you want to do with it. Do you want one hundred per cent? Is seventy-five enough? Have you settled for fifty? What level do you think, honestly, that you have now? Think back a moment to childhood. Are you as healthy as you were then? Healthier?

What is important to you – that you have the stamina to run five miles every morning, that you have flexibility of body gained from an hour's yoga practice every day, or that you get aerobic and anaerobic interval training from an hour on the machines in the gym? Or do you want all three?

On a trip to the USA last year, working in Seattle and San Francisco, with a few restful side trips in between, the whole pattern of what most of us do with our health became very clear. Waking up in my hotel in San Francisco one morning it was so clear to me I just lay in my bed and laughed. I could suddenly see the pattern, the dance we play with our health.

The most amusing part of this dance is that we go on holiday, spend a few weeks feeling wonderful, eat healthy food, lower the stress levels, and come back to work again expecting the feeling of well-being to last. Just think about the balance here; that's two healthy weeks and fifty working weeks each year if you are a Microsoft employee. If you are a Microsoft employee you do that for the first five years, until you are allowed a small amount more time off. In this Microsoft case, that is two hundred and fifty weeks working to ten weeks off.

Isn't that amusing? Where is the dance of balance here? If you are going off on holiday at vast expense to clean air, a clean body and a clearer mind, why would you come back and throw away the money you spent? Because, in a few days this dirty old life can so easily take away all the gain. Would you buy an Armani dress or suit and throw it in the washing machine with harsh detergent the day after you bought it?

I made several changes of pace during this month I had on the West Coast. In Seattle, although working in the corporate arena, I was staying with a friend who is a yoga teacher and lives organically. I ate organic, drank purified water, used organic shampoos and soaps, hiked at weekends and meditated in the sun by a sparkling clean river. My body started to cleanse, the petro-chemical world in which I live in London started to wash out of my system. I started to recognise my childhood body again, feeling clean inside, the sort of feeling you have when you come back from a very expensive health farm, but this was real life.

In San Francisco, my next stop, lying in my bed in the Sheraton hotel, with dust at the edge of the carpets, water that tasted of chemicals and the noise of traffic squealing at the traffic lights having a go at my nervous system, I felt a bit like an oven that had just been cleaned, only to be cooked in soon after. And San Francisco is a whole lot cleaner than other major cities around the world.

What level of external well-being do you want to except? What level of external non-health can you manage? Most people put health on their priority list below their spouses, children and their work. How can that be? Even if they say they don't, in practice, that's what happens. What use are you to anyone without total health? What kind of a weight are you on other people, these spouses, family and companies, if you are unhealthy and stressed?

That is not to say that if you fall out of health, your spouses, family and company shouldn't look after you with tender, loving care, but it is your first responsibility to see that you maintain the best health you know how. It is your responsibility to do everything you can to prevent illness or stress before it happens, to keep your health in balance. Traditionally the Chinese have a good way of thinking about this; they pay their doctors only when they get well. The emperors went one better; if their doctors didn't keep them healthy they were killed. It's the right way around, even if a little drastic!

If you think of the word *aliveness*, ask yourself, do I have that? Does every cell in my body feel alive? Is my heart bursting with cheerfulness, even joy? Are my eyes clear and shining? When I walk, are my knees springing easily; when I carry the shopping do my arms enjoy holding the weight? Is my head clear? If it isn't like this, you don't have full aliveness.

Personally I won't settle for less. I want, when I wake up in the morning, to know that it is good to be alive. And that doesn't mean I'm feeling alive because I have interesting things to do; it means I can feel my heart running along steadily, feel energy going through my body, feel joy just because I'm sitting on the edge of the bed and I feel good.

When clients come to work with me I hardly have to ask them how healthy they are or what they do in the way of exercise. It is written all over them, the way they walk in, the way they sit, the way they move, in their eyes, in their face movements, in their hands, in the way they cross their legs, or talk. From just this I can tell what they do.

As I listen to my clients initially answer the questions that will tell me about their backgrounds, I watch quietly and put a mental percentage on their fitness level. When I find out how fit they are my guess has usually been startlingly accurate. If you look honestly at yourself, listen to your body's complaints and measure your body's successes, you can learn to recognise this for yourself.

TOOLS

- Put a percentage on the level of health you want.

- Put a percentage on your level of aliveness. Is it high enough?

- View your health as the base-line of your life operations.

- Decide what you are prepared to put into your body. A sensible level of organic food would be seventy-five per cent; the next twenty per cent should be as pure as you can practically find; keep an open house on the last five per cent.

- Work out a fitness programme that includes at least two kinds of regular exercise: hiking (walking at different speeds and heights), stretching (yoga, tai chi, etc) and one occasional different exercise so that your body doesn't fall into ritual habits.

THE BODY INFLUENCE

It is important you understand your own body because the wrong recommendations, grafted onto the wrong body, can hinder rather than help. I see people who are told to labour hard in the gym after a long day's work. They don't understand that because of the stressful work they do and the turbulence in their offices they would be better off taking up something like tai chi or yoga and going for walks in the fresh air. I see people who actually need stirring up staying with swimming or yoga only and I want them to do some more aerobic exercise, preferably some interval training or mountain walking, so that their bodies and hearts start moving at faster speeds.

Usually this means setting the person to do the opposite of what is their habit. Think about this for a moment; when you exercise do you usually do the same routines, do you always run but forget to work the top half of your body, do you love the quiet of tai chi done in a classroom and cut the outdoor stuff? To get this back in balance, try doing the opposite of what you usually do for a week and monitor how different you feel.

One of the most important things we can teach our children is to understand what makes their bodies healthy, to value health and wellbeing, to monitor themselves rather than waiting until disaster strikes. We could be teaching them anti-stress techniques before their first exams; even better we could be showing them how not to get stressed when they are very young, how to keep their bodies and minds in the same state in which they arrive as babies. Babies have it right, big smiles, no cares, instinctive cuddling and they wriggle around a lot so their bodies are relaxed.

Think of a small child you know and behave the way he or she does. I have a four-year-old I think of; she smiles a lot, loves talking to people of all ages, is very gentle and very direct. An unusual role model I realise. She hugs me a lot and when she put her head on my lap on a bus journey in Baja, California, I felt an enormous sense of well-being. Her trust in life was tangible and I was warmed by it.

How long since you have done a somersault, a cartwheel or giggled when someone tickled you? All good habits for the adult body. Bring them back into your life. They don't cost anything and they don't take up too much time. They produce the right chemicals in your body and you can do them with other people. These habits don't harm the environment either; in fact, they probably bring cheer to other people around you. My efforts at lop-sided somersaults make my twenty-four-year-old daughter laugh. How could a way of staying in touch with your body be better?

If you look at your body and find some part of it uneven or stiff-looking, then you know something is out of balance. The hunchback of Notre Dame is the obvious case. He was unnoticed and therefore felt unloved, so, quite literally, he grew a chip on his shoulder that visibly said to the world, notice me, I am worth loving. If you look at your body and notice that your neck seems to have shrunk into your shoulders from all the tension you are carrying, then you know that the muscles all down your back are out of balance.

Look around on the beach one day, at the bodies around you. Are they even? Do they look even? I'm not talking Julia Roberts or Elle MacPherson, not asking for public performance perfection. But I am asking you to have your body up and running as easily as possible. That man on the beach over there, the one with one arm slightly shorter than the other; the woman with the bent forward shoulders; that man with the big, stiff-looking back – their imperfections are all easily fixable. They are outward physical manifestations of the not-so-good influences in their lives. They just carry them around, adding to them so gradually with similar behaviour that they don't even notice it.

When you first saw Diana, Princess of Wales at nineteen, for instance, she was carrying few adult worries and was gently willowy. If you looked at her in her early thirties, stunning as she was, she had a ram-rod stiff back. In her bad times she had to carry many tensions on her own and she stored them in her back. In an effort to get away from this massed hurt she carried, she tended sometimes to hold her head a little too high. Holding her head too high resulted from time to time in some not very solid decisions, her head was split off from her heart, the connection lost. The 'Queen of Hearts' inside, the real open-hearted Diana, was then out of equipoise with the Diana who needed desperately to escape her stored hurt feelings.

It's not narcissistic to check on your body and your well-being, it's not self-obsessed to do something about any imbalances you see there. It is rather harsh on yourself to go on letting the influences in your body pull out of balance until you have a major problem. If you can't sit comfortably in your body, you are missing one of the great delights in life.

I was brought up both on mainstream and complementary body disciplines, with a huge slice of body awareness thrown in by my Swiss-German skating teacher in the USA. My grandfather, a medical doctor in New Zealand, wrote health books in the 1920s and 30s. My father, who was a trained osteopath, and who also ran a global pharmaceutical company, cured us with natural cures all my young life. We practised food combining when we were kids, long before the name was ever heard. We were sent to school with bundles of nuts, carrots sticks and fruit; we took high-dose vitamin C as early as the 1950s to get through those foggy, damp English winters we found such a shock after California.

As a result I have a body like a horse. At fifty-three I'm strong and fleet of foot. Yes I went through that very bad patch because of having pushed myself beyond reason, but that was when I ignored the lessons I had been taught. Fortunately my underlying health base was strong enough to build on again. I see so many people who are tired and dispirited. If you were a spirit, I ask them, would you want to be in such an unhealthy body?

TOOLS

- Check your body in a mirror once a week.

- Note any part of it that is out of balance.

- Check your body once a month with a partner; he or she will notice imbalances you are so familiar with that you don't see them.

- If you find anything stiff or uneven, do something about it.

- Doing something about it can be as simple as some full-body and specific stretches or as complicated as a few sessions with the appropriate body-worker.

- Spend some time playing like a child.

- Never ignore what you see. Picking up this imbalance quickly, through either your own efforts or your partner's, is the best route you have to feeling alive and staying well.

THE HEART INFLUENCE

Let's look next at the most hard-worked influence, your heart (for more on the heart, see 'The Power Influence' on page 73). This is the influence that tends to get left out every day for hours and hours. You accept that. You think it is OK to leave it at the corporate door. Let's just think about this for a minute. Why does your briefcase come higher on your list of priorities than your heart?

Do you allow heart-time? At a course for teenagers, my daughter was taught to negotiate with her parents. To get their attention, both she and we were told that if she brought out this small red satin padded heart it meant she really needed to talk to us and we needed to listen fully. A simple device and one I recommend to some of my clients. Heart-time needs to be recognised, given daily time.

Working with someone from the World Bank in a *Life Strategies* session, he said to me, 'Oh, I just want to give up and teach kids.' What was there about teaching kids that he was specially drawn to? 'First,' he said, 'they would be easier.' Then he thought for a moment and answered, 'It's the warmth.'

He was looking for warmth outside himself, to bring towards him, not developing his own warmth in his own heart. Use your own was my advice. 'But I can't,' he said. 'Heads of government aren't interested in heart.' I suggested that a lot of people sitting around the negotiating table might very well want his warmth and he could use as much of it as he could feel in himself. He would then accomplish his work more easily.

Heart connections are the best ones. We all know that, but we just leave our heart at that office door. We are frightened of bringing in our hearts in case we are seen as soft, as bleeding hearts, in case, too, we get them trampled on.

The big-time company I have seen that gets nearest to the heart-stuff is Levi Strauss. In their mission statement they talk about balancing superior profitability, responsibility to society and a work environment that must be 'characterised by fair treatment, teamwork, open communications, personal accountability and opportunities for growth and development'.

The heart-stuff is like anything else in our lives; we have to allow regular time for it, whether at work or play. It can't wait for weekends, nor last thing at night when this much ignored organ is having enough trouble dealing with the day's fatigue.

The sooner you get in touch, physically, emotionally and mentally, with your heart, the less likely you are to have a heart attack. A heart attack comes as a shock only if the person who has had the attack just blindly wore the heart out, and wore it out without even knowing where it was in the body and what it was doing. Getting to know what it feels like, again, is free, not time-consuming and enormously rewarding.

TOOLS

- Check in with your heart in the morning when you get up. 'Good morning, heart. Thanks for your efforts yesterday, heart, I appreciate all that never-ending work you do. It's good to touch you, heart. I'm going to give you a good time today heart.' Touch it. Aaaah! Your own warmth. What a sparkling way to begin. What a good way to prevent heart disease.

THE MIND INFLUENCE

This is the tricky one. It is so hard to keep the mind in order. We place far too much importance on it. We have too much respect for it. We let it run on and on. We aren't very disciplined with it. All that noise and chatter. We allow that voice in our heads to rule, to worry when we are late, to be anxious when we are over-stressed. The mind wants to control us; that is what, physiologically, it is designed to do.

The mind sends out messages all over our body to make us walk, talk, fight or flee. But it is only a set of impulses and we need to be aware of that and keep it in its place.

As an influence the mind leaves a lot to be desired. Think of it as the part of you that will most easily lead you astray if you don't confine it to analysing and organising, and you will be much better off. Your mind is at your soul's command. Do not forget this. If your soul or your spirit, which is the driving force of your soul, submits to your mind, then you live in a very dry place. Living in your head takes you way out of balance; living in balance is keeping your mind under the control of your soul.

TOOLS

- Confine the time you use your mind to when you want it to be working. Stopping it takes some practice but mind-stillness when you are awake is the most peaceful gift you can give yourself.

- Ways to stop your mind are mediation, concentrating on the breath, focusing on the heart.

THE SPIRIT INFLUENCE

Standing on the very white sand beach at Carmel in north California one day I watched a thirties-something man using one of those two-string kites. As he made it dance and play in the sunlight, its bright happy colours sparkling against the blue sky and dark green fir trees, it was almost as if this light-flying, sky-borne toy was his own spirit he had let out to soar. Our spirits are a bit like the kite, let them out for some air and they do dance and soar. As the man played with it, encouraging its wheels and turns, soars and flights, his face started to ease with a natural joy.

When, as a child, I would play a little wildly, my grandmother would stand up for me when my mother wanted to scold. 'It's just high spirits, Tissa my dear,' she used to say in my defence. It's hard to say what the spirit is, in terms we can identify, because we don't know tangibly what it is and where it sits. I know mine has its operations base in my heart because when I am at my happiest I feel a leap of the heart, I feel a gladness there. When I am aware of my spirit being in play, I feel comfortable, sure in what I am doing, I do whatever I am doing with ease, there is no struggle.

There is a lot of talk today about following a spiritual path, as if this were something new. There have always been people who understood the spirit, animists who knew there was a spirit in everything from the grass to the rocks to the trees. Historically from ancient Egypt's all-powerful spirits to Buddhism's evolutionary spirit to the Christian Church's rather negative and subdued spirit, we have been told from on high what the spirit means according to each particular religious institution.

Unless you can feel your spirit in free reign, you are missing something vital. When you are looking at bringing the three fundamental bits of your life together – your mind, your body and your spirit – it is sensible to feel as comfortable with the spirit as you do with your body or your mind. In fact, it is best if they work as a team together.

One of my younger clients was in a muddle about where mind, body and spirit fitted in her life so I gave her a task to help her sort them out. She was to ask each of the three what she should do about an opportunity she was thinking about. The question she was to ask was whether she was going to take a very demanding job she was being offered when she had a small baby in her life and a husband who was also working. 'Sometimes I think I want it and at other times I m sure I don't,' she said. 'Why am I being so chaotic and doubtful?' I explained to her that it was simply that her mind, body and spirit all had a different message for her. She looked a little puzzled but agreed to go away and try.

First she was to ask each of the three parts of her what they thought of this circumstance. Feeling a little stupid, she sat quietly one evening and did as I had requested. Her mind responded with enthusiasm; it revved itself up and gave her an array of options for the problem. Her body sank at the thought; she could feel her energy draining at the idea of putting out more effort. When she got to her spirit, she got a completely different response, 'If you can do this job lightly, and keep time for play, then go ahead.'

When she came back we worked some more with her spirit. Despite belonging to a religion, she had lost touch with what spirit meant for her. 'I think it got submerged when I was on top of a children's slide one day, feeling high-spirited, and my mother yelled out at me to come down or I would get hurt. Somehow I got the message, not her fault, that I couldn't have my own spirit, in fact that it was dangerous to have one. Thank you for helping me get it back. When my spirit told me I needed to go lightly, I realised it was not whether or not I took the job, but how I was going to go about it'.

TOOLS

- Allow your spirit some time in your life.

- Let your spirit remind you to be playful.

THE POWER INFLUENCE

What place do you give power? Do you know what it is? Power is probably the most confusing influence you have in your life. At what level do you want it? At what level are you prepared for the people around you to have it? Are you frightened of it, for yourself or in others when it is directed at you?

We all have people around us who are more powerful than we are, whoever we are. We all sometimes feel powerless. We don't like it so we go to great lengths to avoid putting ourselves into that situation, hold on to our territory, avoid situations, get stubborn, let pride take over, lose the plot in important meetings. The best way to balance power in your world is to know your own, understand it thoroughly and carry it around with you like chocolates in your pocket, a sort of secret trove.

The most interesting point about power is that it is the same for all of us, we just don't realise it. We think it is an intangible. We think some people have power skills and we wonder why there aren't power schools. 'Why can't I be more powerful,' goes the wail. Business schools teach everything else – accountancy, international strategy, finance, marketing, maybe even a little leadership – but not power.

But power is something different. Power is inherent. It is an inner knowledge. This does not mean that you either have it or not. But you do have to be aware of it and develop it. My father, a powerful man himself, said that power was listening, staying quiet and then talking with the quietest voice at the table. Fine for a big man, with a big body. He interspersed it, perhaps once a year, with a little fury, and people knew his measure. The signals were in balance.

I realise now that what he knew, as a birthright, came from his very establishment father, a doctor who had treated and become close to Maoris in New Zealand. He knew from the Maoris that our heart is the best sense we have, that power lies in the heart. I remember him stamping his feet, hitting his heart and singing Maori hakkas in the shower and I could feel the deep sounds vibrating around our cold English bathroom.

I'm not suggesting you stamp in the shower, nor that you stand outside a meeting thumping your heart before you go in. But, if your power influence is not in balance, if you have it one day and not the next, you will always feel unsure.

We talk about someone having a passion for something and going for it. We say someone's heart was in the job. We also know that in physical terms the heart pumps everything that brings life to us around our bodies. But what does give you power is to stop very still for a few minutes a day and listen to your heart. When you get to understand the stillness and quietness of the moment in your heart, you start to understand that power. That's solid power, reliable power, it's free and it's your own.

In this inner power you are impregnable. If you are in touch with the very centre of yourself, how can anyone shake you? How can you fall off balance? Walk into a room with that connectedness and you will take the space. This kind of power isn't something just Winston Churchill or Teddy Roosevelt had; it is open to all of us.

TOOLS

- At any time when you need your power, slow yourself down by breathing softly until you hear the quiet, steady beat of your heart.

- Enjoy the quietness of it for five minutes and feel the power at the centre of your body. Know that this heart power runs all around your body.

- Keep that quietness with you as you go to use your power.

THE EMOTIONS INFLUENCE

Emotions are interesting in the career context. How much do we shut them down at the office door? How much do we choose to let people know how we are feeling? How much do we want to let them out for ourselves?

Emotional behaviour is the influence that differentiates us most from other people. The way our emotions have developed through our lives are unique to us. We are, of course, each of us, quite unique, but it is particularly in the emotional area that we can see our individuality. It is also the emotional area that tends to knock us off our feet from time to time.

Contrary to what many believe, it is not events that knock us sideways but our reactions to them. It is not getting fired that is unpleasant. That is just an event. It is our reaction to it. Working with Prue Leith, I remember asking her how she handled failure. 'Failures? I don't have them. When something goes wrong, I think it through for about a week, work out where the mistakes are and move on swiftly.' She doesn't fall into the emotional pit.

Take divorce. The mechanics of it are quite straightforward. There are a series of moves we have to go through. In Phoenix, Arizona, for example, you can go to an automatic teller machine and in thirty minutes you have every bit of information you need and can fill in all the forms required to get a divorce, all that remains is for a judge to look through them and give them the rubber stamp. But what about the emotional content? What about the feelings – jealousy, rage, insecurity, heartache etc, etc? It is your choice as to how you handle these.

You can deal with them in a week, or a month, or a year or in seven years. Your choice. I know someone who went to Fiji for ten days after his wife said she was leaving. He stayed drunk for most of the time and when he got back he said he felt much less pain. This is not a route I would recommend but he did look at his situation and his hurt and decided to act on it. A woman in Paris is still angry after nine years. She has chosen to keep the hurt and consequently she is finding it impossible to find another relationship.

I was quite emotionally burned at points in my life as a child and when I married I chose someone who had the same sort of background. Where my parents had leaned on me as a go-between, the glue in their marriage, my husband had lived through his parents' terrible divorce. His mother, against a background of revolution in Cairo, threatened the two children that if they saw their father he would kill them. We were fine together for a long time, we just kept moving fast, had a lot of fun, a lot of high life and filled our time with experiences, acquaintances and friends.

We kept each other afloat by the speed of our lives and in the process had very externally rewarding and enviable lives. But, because we hadn't been taught to be emotionally safe and we hadn't had role models who were safe either, we didn't know how to get it ourselves. We had no tools, no strategies for safety. I didn't really know what safety felt like. I went from one exciting event to another, round and round the world. Derek went from one emergency to another; that was what he knew, emergencies were familiar.

By early mid-life we just couldn't live any longer without peace and calm and safety. I was the one who left, but he had shut down, too, to the point where he had closed his business and didn't know what to do next.

What is the range of emotions you favour? At the end of this section you will find some simple exercises that will quickly show you just what you are doing emotionally. It is hard, sometimes, to see how you are handling your emotions. They are so familiar, so ingrained, the behaviour is often so reactive that you just do them. You just do anger or love or jealousy without considering why.

Sometimes I see people who say, 'I don't want to consider my emotions, they are just my emotions.' In a class of mid-career business school participants, one of them challenged me, 'I just love my new girlfriend, why do I want to think about the emotions, that would be inhibiting. I like the spontaneity. If it doesn't work then it just doesn't work. I can always find another girlfriend.' I asked if spontaneity ever got him into trouble with planning at work, and the class laughed – they knew him better than I did and had seen him jumping the gun often in the classroom. One of his team members fed back to him that he needed to think more strategically.

Another participant in the same class had a lot of resentment in him. 'I can't change my work profile at the office, my company wouldn't let me, I know that.' He was resentful of me, too, for suggesting he could and tried to catch me out several times during the lecture.

Resentful was something he quite liked doing. It made anything that happened to him someone else's fault.

The point about carrying negative emotions around with us is that they are very tiring. If I see someone who I think is very emotional I suggest that person walks over to a wall, imagines he or she can off-load the woes on a picture hanger or a hook on the wall. It's a funny little exercise and one that usually brings a smile to the off-loader's face. It would be a wonderful thing to do at the start of any big meeting. Just imagine it, the whole group or team comes in, hangs their troubles on the wall, then sits down with grins on their faces.

One of the best ways to handle emotions is to make an appointment with them. You are worrying about something, for example, and you can't keep a clear head. It's no use saying that the emotion isn't there and going on stoically; it will get worse and worse, growing below the surface until it affects your behaviour. Just say to yourself, 'I can't deal with this now but I will do it at eight this evening for half an hour.' If you slot in a time, you know there is an outlet and you can stay clear and peaceful until then.

Making an appointment with yourself allows you to stay steady. Give your emotions the same level of attention you would credit a business meeting. Give them defined time and space. If this sounds too clinical, think for a minute; these emotions are as much a part of you as your muscles and you give those time in the gym or out walking, don't you?

When my father committed suicide my mother didn't want anyone to know, so I buried my grief and guilt and went on travelling around the world in my journalist job, with an enthusiastic smiling face. A year later I woke up one morning and couldn't get out of bed. I suddenly felt deeply depressed. If someone close to you commits suicide it is the most aggressive act he or she can do because you have no way of answering. The person is gone, having removed him or herself from you and you can do nothing about it. I felt guilty because I hadn't stopped my father, powerless because I thought if I had been a better person he wouldn't have gone.

My self-belief went and I had a whole load of anger because he had left without saying goodbye. Instead of dealing with this week by week, as time progressed, I had to deal with it all at once and it wasn't easy. I was unsteady for several months, unsure of my ability to deal with my own or other people's emotions. In fact, because I blamed myself, I thought I was harmful to people and closed my heart off. I didn't know I had done that, but I certainly didn't feel very loved through that period, nor did I probably give much love.

Had I dealt with it by talking to friends, spending a little time every day to feel it through, this unsteadiness wouldn't have happened. Emotions are best kept in a structured shape, handled bit by bit.

The happier emotions need dedicated time, too. I often ask my clients if they have celebrated a success. Particularly in England, they just nod modestly and say little. If you don't give the time to pat yourself on the back you don't get enough good feelings. Celebrating is a ritual; it marks for you what you have done well, focuses on your finer points, so that you add this to your body life-prints.

If you feel too often what hasn't worked, then that's what you actually feel in your mind and body, the emotion of disappointment or failure. Feeling the good stuff needs to take more time than feeling the bad stuff. This is how you get the right balance. It is as simple as that. Feeling the good stuff is not conceit, it's just a very effective way of living.

We tend to operate within a fairly small range of emotions. If you think of your emotions as radio channels you can dip in and out of, you can see the pattern, we all have our favourite programmes on a few favourite channels. Imagine you have just bought a new digital radio with all the world bands and tune into your emotions in the same way as you would surf these channels. Some emotions will be as unfamiliar as Chinese radio, others as solid as the BBC. Would you like to tune into that faint one, the joy emotion, and tune it up louder? What about wonder, how long since you have felt pure wonder? Serenity? Adoration? Exhalation?

Emotions are like anything else you want in your life. Unless you focus on the good ones, you get only the middling or bad ones. Catch that fleeting moment of happiness and grow it into something big.

I am surprised there aren't whole books on the joy emotion. Joy is what we need most. Joy is sharing something, giving someone something and seeing their face light up, joy is a hug that is full of warmth, joy is breaking a record, succeeding at something new. Joy is one of the biggest components of aliveness. We say there isn't enough joy in the world but we don't give ourselves enough time to have it. We almost think it is not something to expect in our day-to-day lives; it is an emotion we expect to feel at airports when we meet someone who has been away, at the birth of a baby, at weddings, when we have good sex.

I was working with a client this morning who came to me with a career decision. We had talked through this for three sessions; each time I asked him to go away and answer certain questions that were designed to trigger some new thinking in him. At this, the forth session, he said he was beginning to get the concept of building a new role for himself. I still saw no passion, no sparkle. He was being careful to the extreme, not showing any enthusiasm, he was actually fighting me not to show any enthusiasm, not in an unpleasant way but in a subconsciously determined way. He is in his late thirties, he doesn't have a relationship, or rather has just finished a somewhat upsetting one. He works for a transnational company, between two European markets.

I asked him what his friends feed back to him. 'They say I'm too serious,' he answered. I told him he isn't going to make any new decisions, find new avenues, until he opens up his heart and his emotions. He grinned a little sheepishly. 'In fact,' I said, 'only about half of you is alive. That's the half we have to work with and expand, then you can decide where to go in your career.'

We built a programme for him for two months – he had to make some decisions for his company in three months' time. For two months he was to do anything he could think of that wasn't what he usually did. He was to take up scuba diving, start hiking, join groups of people and start doing yoga. He started having massages two weeks previous to this, as a result of our third session, and moved on to a healthier diet. He put tennis on the back burner for a bit because it wasn't getting him fit and he knew it too well.

He had two business days away in two different European countries and I suggested he found time to do something really silly or funny within those days. In Madrid he could go to see a Velázquez and laugh at the pompous little girl in the *Las Meninas* painting. In Paris he might skip down the road for two hundred yards. They do it in the movies and we love the movies so why not do it ourselves?

The point of introducing these changes was to start to shift his very still energy around. We carry our emotions in our bodies; our brains send emotional messages to the satellite-like receptors around the body. I wanted him to send some different messages around the circuit and to do that I had to shake him up. He wasn't going to find joy until he shifted the caution message. His receptors were frozen on caution.

The opposite of joy, of course, is depression. Depression is exactly what it says, depressed, i.e. held-down, emotions. There are many treatments and many words said in the lifting of it, in the lifting of your spirit again until you feel joy. We all get depressed sometimes. Because we move so fast in our current world there are more and more of us feeling lousy. We haven't been able to keep our spirits high enough in this harsh, over-stimulated, over-polluted, over-noised time.

This is one of the reasons why there has been such an extraordinary rise in complementary or alternative medicines, in the number of people going to spiritual healers, aromatherapy, massage, colonic irrigation, etc. One of the biggest social changes of the 1990s has to be that so many people have needed some kind of emotional support outside the family.

We know at the bottom of our psyches that we are taking too much on; we feel the emotions come welling up and when they won't stay tidily down, we just push them out of the way. We need to stop to manage ourselves before we get to the point where we need support. There are no real figures on the complementary medicine industry, on how much is earned by the whole gamut of emotional, mental and physical therapy, because so much of it is earned in black money, but the hunger for gentleness, peace and for feeling some of the softer emotions now has a life of its own. This hunger will grow bigger and bigger until there is a better balance of the harsh and the gentle.

TOOLS

- On the next two pages there are most of the emotions we deal with on a day-to-day basis. Before you look at the words, ask yourself whether you think there are more happy or more unhappy emotions. Your answer will tell you where the balance lies. Think through these words for a few moments and then answer the questions and make the lists suggested on page 83. This will allow you to sort out the emotions you use, prioritise some you would like more often and get rid of some of the more obsessional or habitual ones that are stopping you from living more easily in balance.

SORROW SADNESS BESOTTED OBSESSIVE

SHAME POSSESSIVENESS   THE BLUES

INSECURITY   UNHAPPINESS   SADNESS

MELANCHOLY   DESPONDENCY   GLOOM

DEJECTION GRIEF MISERY HOSTILITY

PARANOIA GUILT CONTRITION MISGIVING

HESITANCE DOUBT SCEPTICISM SUSPICION

MISTRUST   CYNICISM   PESSIMISM

SUSPICION   DEJECTION   DEPRESSION

WORRY DISQUIET DISTRESS WOE AGONY

ANGUISH TORMENT PAIN DISTRESS

ALARM   FRIGHT   AWE   DREAD

APPREHENSION CONSTERNATION DISMAY

PANIC   FRIGHT   TERROR   HATE

DISGUST   AVERSION   RANCOUR

MALEVOLENCE REVENGE HORROR SHOCK

WONDER   ADMIRATION   RESPECT

AMAZEMENT SURPRISE STUPEFACTION

DEFERENCE HOMAGE LOVE ATTACHMENT

DEVOTION   AFFECTION   ARDOUR

FONDNESS PASSION ADORATION PATIENCE

CALM   SERENITY   PLACID   TRANQUIL

GOOD-NATURED   SEDATE   COMPOSED

GENIAL   MELLOW   KINDNESS

COMPASSION GENEROSITY BENEVOLENCE

OPEN-HANDEDNESS GIVING FORBEARANCE

HAPPINESS   SATISFACTION   MERRIMENT

GLADNESS   RAPTURE   BLISS   ECSTASY

TRANQUILLITY   EXHILARATION   ELATION

CHEERFUL LIGHT-HEARTED CONTENTMENT

DELIGHT JOY EXALTATION CONCERN

CARING   LUST   DESIRE

- Think through these pages of emotions for a few moments.

- Ask yourself: on which ones you are out of balance? Do you leave certain ones at home? Are you conscious of the ones you leave at the office door? Are you depriving yourself of any? Are there any you would like to banish? Are there any you use obsessionally, such as unhappiness?

- Notice that there are more words for negative emotions that positive ones. List the ten negative emotions and the ten positive emotions you use most often.

- Make a list of the ten you would like to banish.

- Make a list of the ten you want more of.

- Make a list of the ten positive ones you haven't tried in your life yet. Try each of these on for size, perhaps one a day. For example, if passion has been missing, keep that in your heart and mind for a day, get familiar with it and then when you know it better, if you want more of it, it becomes simple to bring it into your life.

THE RELATIONSHIP INFLUENCE

Balancing a relationship, is there anything more complicated to do? Are relationships the highest priority in our lives? Is loving someone and keeping the human survival instinct intact the thread we need in our lives to feel we are OK? Do we place far too much importance on our relationships, expect this wonderful other person to supply us with all the things we don't have in ourselves?

How much time do you spend working at your relationship? And I don't mean arguing. Do you sit down and consider what you want to have together? Or throw ideas at each other on the run? Is there any strategy in your relationship? Do you feel you are in balance with each other? And what would that balance be for you? If you imagine your relationship as an ongoing dance of balance, where is the Centre Point of that dance? What is it that keeps the two of you in balance?

I was married for six months when British *Vogue* offered me the job as travel editor. I had gone for a junior fashion job and the rather daunting editor Beatrix Miller had suddenly pointed at me in the interview and said, 'You can be the travel editor.' Maybe it was the hunger in my eyes, maybe it was my skating travels: I certainly didn't know what travel editors did.

By the time I had walked the fifteen minutes home, I was pretty sure I wanted to do it. The fact that I had only been married six months didn't occur to me until I got through the front door of our tiny London mews flat. The fact that I had married a Middle Easterner, and that this job, which sounded so appealing to me, might not appeal to him for his new wife only hit me as I sat down on the sofa. This was certainly going to upset our balance.

We sat down and talked about it and came to an agreement that it was too good an opportunity to miss. He did feel apprehensive about it, though. We decided that, one, we would talk about it in six months, at which point he would have the right to say he hated my doing it, and we would consider my leaving or whatever, and that, two, if I was away too much, he had the right to put up his hand and wave it for attention.

We had set in some strategic structure within which to contain what could have become an unbalanced situation leading to the possible break-up of a fragile new marriage. Setting in that structure didn't mean it ruled our lives but it did mean we had something to work with as the situation developed. The funny thing about the situation was that although Derek did wave his hand from time to time and say, 'What about commissioning that story and staying home for a bit?' it was I who decided in the long run that I had been away enough.

Here's a fun exercise to do with your partner. I know it sounds a little strange to ask you both to do a pie chart of the way you each balance your lives, but it is a very good way of showing you both just how different or how similar your lives are. As you can see from the illustration opposite, it's truthful, too, in a clear diagrammatic form; you can't fudge it the way you can with words.

I find couples are usually surprised at how unbalanced their mutual lives look. Sometimes when I see these pie charts, I wonder how the two people manage to communicate at all, their life-patterns are so different. Often, when doing this exercise, they do not draw in any time for each other and when I ask why, they answer, 'We live together, that's all the time.' 'No good,' I say, 'that's fragmented time;

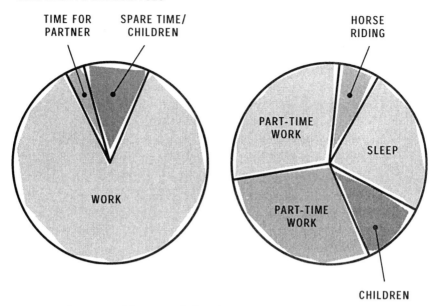

TIME FOR PARTNER   SPARE TIME/ CHILDREN   HORSE RIDING

PART-TIME WORK   SLEEP

WORK

PART-TIME WORK

CHILDREN

you need to set aside mutual time.'

A woman in an international telecoms company was working in another country from her husband and had been doing so for nearly a year. 'I see him quite often,' she had said defensively. When she drew her pie chart there was a tiny, tiny sliver of time they spent together. She had convinced herself she could do this separation and pushed away the missing of him. When she saw the visual reality of it, all her unhappiness came flooding to the top. Her defensiveness had covered her unease. We worked out a new plan for her, in stages, which she took to her bosses for negotiation, so that she would have more immediate time at home and within three months be back living there.

You need to book regular time with your partner. Peter Carey, the Australian Booker Prize winning author of *Oscar and Lucinda*, and his theatre-manager wife had a baby in their early forties. Right from the start they booked a babysitter every Tuesday evening, so that they would continue to have their own time and not let the balance swing helplessly towards baby life. Because it was set in every week they found something interesting to do or they had a wonderful, quiet meal together.

Most important of all with the relationship influence is the agreement you make with each other before you get married. It isn't enough to feel the chemistry, make the two sentences of vows at the church and then get on with it. Love, honour and obey, or not obey, are a little vague for the 1990s. I'm not suggesting a financial agreement as a necessity but it does help when you divorce. Because my husband and I jointly owned everything, it was technically easy to split it up when we parted. My divorce cost $250.00. I just filled in a green form.

If you sit down, at regular intervals, during your courting and engagement time and talk through what you believe, what your values are, what you want out of your life and how you see the future, you may either avoid the wrong marriage or set in some useful guidelines in the right one.

We tend to think that if we are drawn to someone that it will all work out. Unfortunately the biological signals in our body are really basic ones, put there to insure the survival of the human race. We weren't supplied with a strong enough analytical countermechanism to counterbalance all these survival chemicals. Neither do we listen to our parents much any more, so that's another set of discussions that are missed out on.

A young couple I worked with thought they had everything in common; they had known each other for a year before they married. When they came back from their honeymoon, they both went into independence in a big way and picked up their old interests. 'But he/she always wanted to do everything together,' they each wailed. During courtship they had both given up their individual interests for the being-together phase. 'I'm not interested in my flying any more,' he had said, 'I'd rather be with you.' 'I've grown out of hiking holidays, she had said, I d rather be with you.'

Suddenly they discovered they was nothing much they liked doing together. Their weekends were spent apart. She hated flying and he wanted the freedom of the air, the inspiration of big horizons. She wanted her feet on the ground, the contact with the earth, the nice easy pace, the companionable talks of hiking. They had just assumed their need to be together would overcome anything and focused only on the feelings. By the time I saw them they were spending only two evenings a week together, few weekends, and were quite relieved to do only that. They came because they were on the way to splitting up.

What we had to do was establish some new common ground, a safe place for them to start to talk and some new territory for them to move ahead on. If you start to do something new together you avoid bringing in all the old baggage. But we had to find what that was. Neither wanted to lose the old territory. We looked at all their influences, individually and together. Earth and sky, they each have one of those, I thought, so what about something that includes both, say bird-watching around the world, which is sky and earth, but which is new territory for both? Or something to do with water, which is further from both? Sailing, power-boating, swimming?

In times when a relationship has come unstuck or become a little dull, find something new to do together that neither of you have done before. Doing this means you take a clean slate for both of you and will bring in less of the habits that you know so well about each other. You are not allowed to judge each other either. No '*Why can't you get this right?*' It's also much funnier if you do something a little unusual, out of character; and if you laugh together, the wrinkles in the relationship will soon start to disappear.

One couple I worked with, who found their lives had become almost entirely separate after eleven years, decided to take up yoga. When they started to work with their bodies, they could see very clearly their differences and what was happening to them. In yoga class she could do all the flexible movements and he the ones that required strength. She was good with her legs and hips, he with his chest and shoulders. At first he kept saying to her, 'Of course you can do handstands,' and she kept wondering why he couldn't do the body twists.

Through their bodies, they could read to each other what they were doing in their lives. They could see clearly the way they were going about their individual lives, without any words. He was running a division of a company and had the tough, powerful upper body he had developed to maintain this pursuit. She was working in education where she had needed all the pliancy and versatility at her disposal. Neither was right and neither was wrong.

What both of them could do with was a bit of what the other had. She needed more upper body strength to achieve all the yoga exercises and he needed to develop more flexibility. 'We have been running our lives thinking it was acceptable that we were so polarised but getting to feel really isolated from each other. Now we can see ourselves growing together as we each develop the other side of ourselves.'

One of the difficulties people in relationships have is not to lean towards each other. You meet someone and they have all the attributes you want. He laughs a lot, for instance, and she is very gentle. So you lean towards each other and gobble up that gentleness or that sense of humour.

The trouble is that what you really need is not to get that gentleness or that sense of humour from the other one, but to recognise that when you want something in someone else, what you really want is to feel it inside yourself. So if you meet the guy with the sense of humour, take a look at yourself, how is your sense of humour? If you like her warmth and smile, could it be that you need to find more of that in yourself? You can't go on for the rest of your life expecting your partner to smile for you when you are sad, or be gentle for you when you are feeling tough.

Neither can you neglect these large chunks of yourself. If you have a coldness inside, you welcome someone who comes towards you with a lot of warmth. There's that old expression – being warmed by someone's love – but, of course, you have to warm that person back. Too often when the warmth dies and the cold appears, you tend to think it is the other person who is being cold. In reality it is you that needs to give out your own sunshine. Why should others have the responsibility to keep offering you their sunshine for the rest of their lives?

If you know what you are in balance with and what you are out of balance with, you are then clear on what you are bringing into a relationship. Obviously you can't wait until you are perfectly balanced, before you join up with someone, nor can you wait until you find someone who is perfectly balanced. An Australian woman living in Singapore is doing just that and she has been waiting eleven years. 'When I've got myself all sorted out the right person will appear. I don't want a man who isn't sorted out.'

Your responsibility is to be aware of your own dance of balance, feel yourself placed at the Centre Point of it, recognise your balanced state and try to get back there as quickly as you can, as often as you can. If two of you are going to dance this balance together, put the awe and wonder at the centre of what you are doing and make sure you plan to keep it in place. When you understand your own dance of balance you can more easily understand someone else's. If you can tell this new someone in your life how yours works, that person can more easily tell how his or hers work.

It is with the awe and wonder, the same awe and wonder we credit the stars at night or a marvellous opera performance, that we can build the separate form that is a relationship. Unless we build this thing, this other, this connection, we just stay as two entities, oscillating and unconnected at any deep level, two bundles of energy on the loose.

Because we have so little in the way of extended families and so few role models in the home, we grow up feeling alone and isolated and this makes it harder to understand what a strong connection, this other form, can be. It was simple for a cave child, he or she just had to sit around and watch parents, uncles and aunts parade their roles.

When actress Gwyneth Paltrow and Brad Pitt became engaged in what appeared to be the prefect Hollywood romance, Paltrow said that for the first time she felt complete. What she was actually feeling was the comfort of a twenty-something, who for the first time since she had gone though those years of childhood and teenage isolation, was feeling close to someone again, a closeness she had probably lost before she was three.

How awful for her when she breaks up because she loses that sense of completeness; she is lost and alone and isolated again. No one should be able to take this completeness away from us, it is something we must have for ourselves. When a partner comes along, and we choose to engage with that person, we have the chance to get to know more about ourselves; we get to dance with ourselves as well as dance with another.

If Paltrow had not set the completion expectation so high she might not have been so disappointed. If she had spent more time identifying what she needed to supply herself with, then she would have had something more whole to offer her mate.

The important bit to remember is that we are all made up of the same qualities, we just have them in different allowances. We can choose to develop one and atrophy another at any time. We will certainly be much more successful if we have all our own qualities in a better balance. When we have our own balance finely tuned we are in a good position to dance the dance of balance with another person. This is a dance of equals and it is much more fun.

The next exercise I go through with couples is asking them to draw how they would like their lives to look in five years. They do it together in front of me. They don't look at each other's until they are finished.

The first two drawings below are very similar; this couple want the same things, they just haven't taken the time to work out the steps to get there. If this is your case, then set some meetings in with each other, week by week; treat each other with the respect you would give a business meeting or a hospital appointment. What makes these meetings work is that you prepare for them in the time leading up to

the meeting, you arrive with a clear agenda. Also, you know you are going to be listened to and that takes any potential conflict out of the circumstances.

The second couple, in the illustration opposite, want something quite different, not surprising since she is in a very large corporation and he works from home. They have been married for two years and have had quite a few problems. I had been working with the wife on her life planning and we decided to ask her husband to come in. I worked with him on his own a few times and then with both of them together. I asked them first to draw their individual life-prints. His is solitary, hers has lots of people in it. And that's exactly how they are running their lives, staying the way they were before they got married.

In relationships you need to play with the way your lives are. The components of your lives are there to rearrange. Nothing is fixed. There are an infinite number of possibilities of how you could run your relationship, why not try a few more of them?

The things we do together startle me constantly. We tug and we

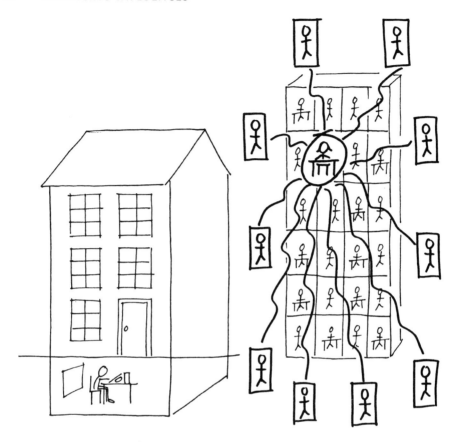

pull, we take stances, we get angry and we fight. There is something very simple to do here. Play with the elements of your relationship as if your were playing a board or computer game. Play around with it until it is absolutely unfamiliar. Then stand back and re-invent it keeping what you want of the old and the new. This relationship is the most time-consuming influence of your life, so make sure it influences that life in the way you want.

TOOLS

- Book appointments with each other.

- Be sure you are not leaning on the other person for something that is missing in yourself.

- Give each other a whole day. The person whose day it is gets to choose everything, all day. This is the best way I know to feel close to someone.

- Take time to play with components of your relationship as if you are playing a computer game; in this way you become aware of all the possibilities you can have.

- Play around with your relationship in this way until it is absolutely unfamiliar and you don't recognise it.

- Then stand back and together invent a new form, keeping what you want of the old, then banish some of the old.

THE TOTALLY NEW INFLUENCE

So far you have looked at the key influences in your life. On each of these you can easily put a name or a label. These vital players in your life, though, cannot be set in an appropriate balance until you add the totally new, something new that will keep you from concentrating on what you already know.

One of the themes you will notice throughout the book is my suggesting you take time for yourself, every day. This is particularly important when you want to bring something totally new into your life. 'I haven't time for anything more,' I hear. 'I'm too tired to add anything else. I've been wanting to learn French for years but haven't done it,' I hear.

At the same time as I started writing this book I took up sailing, signed myself up for a Royal Yachting Association Competent Crew course. A friend said I was mad, I shouldn't take my attention away from the book. I understood what she was saying as I had only five months to write it and I had a practice to keep going. But I also knew that I needed something new to do both to keep my mind fresh and to stop myself from working too long hours. If I just went on with all the old interests it would be easy to write more hours at a stretch than was necessary. I also wanted to ensure there was a sense of aliveness all the way through. I already knew about writing, how to do that, so I wanted regular newness. I wanted a parallel challenge, albeit a relaxing one, to dilute the importance of writing the book.

Unless you actually programme in the time for the totally new, how does it find a place in your life? Unless you regularly set time you will fill it with the old and the nearly new. Even if you don't yet know what you want to do with this time, take the two or five or ten hours and fill them with thinking about your new.

The professor of international business at the London Business School sets aside one day a week to keep in touch with new developments in his field. Without that time, he says, he doesn't have anything challenging to offer his students and his consultancy clients. This policy enables him to charge several thousand pounds a day.

Bringing in the totally new is not doing something you have had a mind to do for ten years. It is something you have never done. It must be something shiningly new, something that, when you think of it, brings a sparkle to your eyes.

I worked with someone who had Chronic Fatigue Syndrome (CFS) and this person was quite determined to stay where she was, exhausted. I asked her one day what new thing would bring a sparkle to her eyes and caught her unawares. 'I'd like to have a season ticket on the mountain chairlifts in Switzerland,' she sparkled. An interesting answer because what she actually wanted to do as something totally new was something she had the strength for at that moment.

The only way this woman was going to find a different today than her CFS was if she added something shiningly new. To add something shiningly new she had to clean out one or two of yesterday's influences. She had to let go some of the exhaustion influences that were holding her down. Seen as a simple barter, just one or two items, she was able to move to the new without having to let go too much of her familiar agony at once. The totally new is often the only avenue that is sparkling enough to make the effort to head for.

TOOLS

- Progressively set yourself time for the totally new.

CHAPTER SEVEN

BALANCING THE PAST AND THE FUTURE

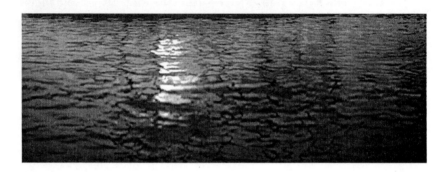

To get the future you want, you have to do several things. Sift through your unachieved ideas so that you sort out the ideas you haven't acted on and get rid of the ones that are no longer relevant. You can then keep the important and useful elements and put them together in a form which would be useful to you today.

If you clear away the mental and emotional weight from yesterday you release tension and tiredness, leaving you secure and without fear of the future. Allow the dead stuff to fall away and you can re-invent yourself in your body and mind's newer territory.

It is important to understand the habits that have become your drivers, so that you fully grasp the difference between your war zones, your success habits and your inherent power.

When you realise that the future you want uses everything you have already done, you will see the richness you have to offer. Keeping your past and your future in balance also gives you the sure footing to revel in today.

We often sit in today and think we can't move ahead because we are carrying too much mental and emotional weight. We tend to carry our histories like burdens on our shoulders without noticing anything but the tension. I remember my ex-husband saying to me in my thirties, when I was having trouble making a change, 'You're just a like a Ferrari parked in a garage with the door shut. You're sitting there, revving the engine, but going nowhere. What about opening the door and just backing out?'

Taking his analogy a little further, if you burn your wheels for too long, you wear out the tyres. We do this when we are running to stand still, we wear out our energy. Our bodies and minds get tired trying to repeat the same patterns. And when that happens we think we are no good any more, that we are failures, that we can't do what we used to be able to do very well. From this a huge insecurity arises and we become too scared to move either forwards or backwards.

I know two men, one in his fifties, one in his sixties, who are having a lot of trouble balancing their pasts and their futures. Although they are of different ages the importance of understanding this past/future balance is the same for any age. The American, who has an oil field in South America along with a few other successful, mostly high-revenue businesses, has just broken both ankles in a sports accident. The other, English, a respected figure in London's financial investment world, has just bashed his head devil-karting down a mountain while on holiday with his thirteen-year-old twin sons.

Both these men, equally fearless in business, are deeply frightened of moving into their futures. Neither will stop to look at his life; they both just keep pushing ahead. The American has very effectively brought himself to a halt, at the moment he can't go much further than the side of his bed. The Englishman has this wonderful flag on his pate that says I took a headlong halt. They are both stuck in the past, a past of fast achievement, measurable success and control over the world around them.

The trouble for both of them is that they have finished the phase they have been in but they won't recognise it. So they are running around, hitting the same war zones, out of balance with their present and not aware of a new kind of future. 'I want more peace and quiet, less rushing around,' the Englishman said to me last month.

The next time he talked to me it was from his mobile phone, walking down one of London's busiest streets, half an hour late for a film with one of his children, having just hurried home after work to pack his suitcase for his newly taken-on monthly board meetings in America. He keeps taking on a new future that is the same as his today. So he just gets more out of balance. A fleet air arm pilot from age eighteen to twenty-six, he is still throwing himself at danger in his fifties, so he tips the balance yet more towards the past. He makes me smile. He doesn't see that to get some balance in his life, to get that 'peace and quiet', he has to start trying new pursuits.

'Peace and quiet' doesn't come by racing down a mountain. But he can't see it; he thinks it will come just by having the idea in his head. Peace and quiet will come if he starts doing peace and quiet. But when you are stuck in the past, that's all you see.

When you continually look forwards, you are not focusing on today. Getting the right balance between the past and the future allows you to sit comfortably in today. The American nursing his ankles needs to open up a future that is important enough to him so that he feels secure enough to jettison today. He certainly isn't comfortable in today.

He has had some thirty years of a successful business career but he doesn't see that he could have the same kind of success doing something completely different. He is busy doing more of the same, but there comes a point when we have done enough of the past and it doesn't work well any more.

His fear of the future is greater than his fear of hurting himself so he is out of balance. In this position he is first emotionally and then physically hurting himself. To build himself an equally interesting and challenging future, he has to decide his future is more important than his past. He has to realise that his fear of not having as good a future as his past is getting him into trouble.

Fear of the future, that is not doing the future, is more likely to kill than walking into the future. People who get heart attacks are usually the ones who keep pushing at the same tasks. Their emotional hearts are so fearful of changing that their minds keep engaging them at the same task. Their hearts die for two reasons: first, because they haven't allowed themselves the hope of something new, and second because the stress of forcing the heart to meet the same mind and body challenges over and over, whatever they are, wears it out.

As my grandmother used to say, 'A little bit of everything is what you need in life.' And now that we need to plan for longer lives we have time for a little bit of everything; a little bit of everything is not only what we can have but what we will have to have – choice is becoming a must. Staying on one narrow, over-focused track, wearing out at seventy, a year or two after retiring, was the old way. Now that we have this longer future we can have the joy of several different lives in one. The sooner my two friends see this the better off they are going to be.

The sooner they realise that they can have as interesting a life over the next thirty years as they have had in last thirty, the sooner they will realise that to start the next stage of their future they may have to start to do something that they are not as good at as their current circumstance – but at something which they may even become better. Then they can stop bashing their heads and breaking their ankles.

A very attractive, very bright, mid-thirties female in public relations is also stuck in today. She has a good job in London and just added to her life a man who lives in Italy. She doesn't speak Italian. Her career here is fine, her past is fine. Her today is a little muddled. Her new man is quite well off and likes her a lot. She finds him warm, caring and thoughtful towards her. It all sounds quite wonderful and it is. But she is caught between yesterday and tomorrow and feels very uncomfortable. They get on well when she visits him, but she misses her life in London. They don't get on so well in London because he feels a little lost. Cross-border love, it's happening to more and more of us. With two clear pasts, how do they move to a future, how do they get out of the rather bewildering see-saw they are in? Where's the equilibrium for them?

First, it is sensible to look at a future that contains some new central element that belongs to neither of their pasts. They need to break the lock they are in that asks *yours or my past?*, because that's what they are taking about at this point, even if they don't know it. If they can view their possible future in the same way they would view the merging of the two businesses they work in, the process would look simpler (see overleaf). It will also help to take some of the emotion out of the thinking.

We all carry lots of emotions from our past and they aren't much use to us. Past emotions are a bit like products that are past their life-

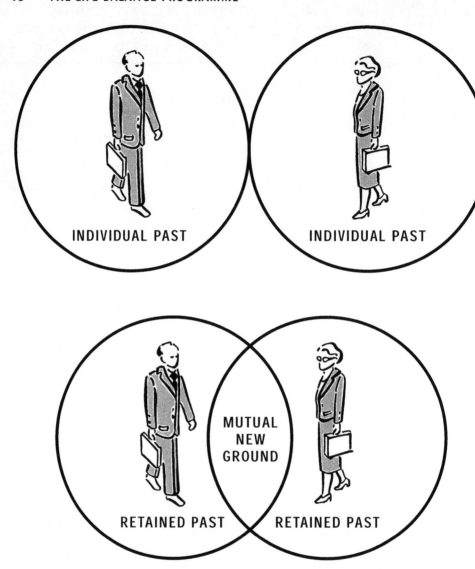

cycle; the best thing to do with them is decide on a useful shelf-life
and then get them out of the market to make room for the new product.

You can use Microsoft as a master example of this. The company
brings out a leading-edge product and the rest of the market has to
arrange itself around it. Also, the product is usually so startlingly new
that everyone else in the company, regardless of their particular patch,

finds it irresistible. Other projects are happily discarded. The new product becomes the central force in the company's strategy. On the leading edge of technology, no one hangs on to the past. Think of your own past and future in the same way.

My client and her man had to do several things to sort out their pasts and their dilemma:

- First, they each listed which of the bits of their past were non-negotiable and which were negotiable.
- Second, they had to find their own new product. The new product in people terms is the new stuff you want to do. In this couple's case it is a kind of future they hadn't thought of when they were busy trying to hold on to their individual pasts.

To get past their pasts they have to invent themselves a new future that has at its centre something they do together that neither has done before. When they have this in place it gets much easier to let go of most of the non-negotiables. The non-negotiables, the bits they need to discard, become surprisingly unimportant in the new territory. To get the balance between the past and future they need to build the sort of future neither of them has thought of.

They didn't fall for each other just so they could give up all of their lives for the other. They probably fell for someone so different because they themselves were out looking for something new, exotic. And two such intelligent people can have a lot of fun inventing a new kind of strategic alliance that sits happily, comfortably in both circumstances.

The challenge and the fun lies not in getting the other to do what you do; what's new in that for you? You would still be doing the same things, only having someone else around doing them with you who isn't as good at doing them as you. The fun lies in designing something together that brings a separate and mutual life to the situation.

TEN UNACHIEVED IDEAS

I want you to think of *ten unachieved ideas* in your life, ten somethings you have wanted to do at some stage of your life but have never got around to doing. The exercise looks simple but it will take you a long way towards balancing your past and your future.

Doing this exercise allows you to root around in your past within a simple structure so that you sort out the ideas you haven't done and get rid of the ones that are no longer relevant. You can't then keep the important and useful elements so that you can put them together in a form which would be useful to you today.

These ideas can be as silly or as serious as you like and can come from any period of your life, from childhood through to your life right now. For example, a client of mine, in his forties, still hankered after being a stand-up clown. When we looked at this idea carefully, we found that while he didn't actually want to be a stand-up clown any more, the element he did want to keep out of this long-held yearning was to speak out more. We put this in as a major force in the planning we did together.

The exercise:

- First you need to list your ten unachieved ideas.
- Then write a few lines by each one about why you wanted to do it.
- Then write down why you didn't do it.
- List the elements you want to keep.
- The two examples below show how to do this.

FAST-TRACK, EARLY-THIRTIES MAN: TEN UNACHIEVED IDEAS

Here is an example of a fast-track, early-thirties married man. This is his list. This man took a year off when he was thirty-four. He earned a lot of money and could afford to do this easily. At the end of the year he had seen a lot more of his wife and child, which he had enjoyed. 'I sat in my square in Chelsea (London) and talked to the women looking after their children. I loved it.' But at the end of the year he hadn't found a new direction so he went back to the same kind of job.

He wasn't very happy doing the same job again and felt he had just gone from one extreme to the other and back again. He wasn't very happy either that he was still watching television late at night to try to relax, long after his wife had gone to bed.

When he brought me his list, saying, 'I couldn't get to ten unachieved ideas, I can't think of any more' I could see they were absolutely representative of someone in his fast-track thirties – they were activity based and achievement oriented. The fact that he couldn't get the whole ten was a clear indication that he wasn't able to think of anything much outside his work. None of these unachieved ideas was difficult and none was really going to be part of a new career for him. This exercise showed too that he was stalled in his mind about a different kind of work and lifestyle.

1. Play tennis

- *Wanted to because*: Get fit, see more people
- *Didn't because*: I did buy a tennis club membership but I was always too busy

2. Buy a bike

- *Wanted to because*: Get fit ˙
- *Didn't because*: I didn't know where to go, going around the square would be boring

3. Take another trip to Africa

- *Wanted to because*: It's inspirational
- *Didn't because*: No time

4. Do an outward bound course

- *Wanted to because*: Get fit, challenge myself
- *Didn't because*: No time

5. Turn off the TV

- *Wanted to because*: Sit there on my own, wife goes to bed first, waste of time, lazy habit
- *Didn't because*: didn't know what else to do

6. Be a film critic

- *Wanted to because*: Would like to write about film
- *Didn't because*: Don t know how

7. Overcome fear of public speaking

- *Wanted to because*: Do some with work, very well, but get very frightened beforehand
- *Didn't because*: What would be the use?

8. Learn another language

- *Wanted to because*: Talk to more people
- *Didn't because*: Work such long hours, no time

What we did take from his list, though, were the missing elements of needing to meet different kinds of very bright people and bring in the kind of challenges that would exercise both his mind and his body. He needed much more stimulation than he was getting to pull him out of a state that was very low on inspiration.

EARLY-FORTIES MAN: TEN UNACHIEVED IDEAS

Another example of this ten unachieved ideas exercise is an early-forties male who came to me because his company, having given him a superb assessment two years before, changed their recent assessment and asked him to look for another job.

1. Practise law

- *Wanted to because*: It is safe, like the intellectual discipline, want recognition.
- *Didn't because*: Long training, have a family, fear of another failure

2. Start own ski-wear business

- *Wanted to because*: Like skiing, want own business, freedom, fun
- *Didn't because*: Didn't find the right partner

3. Be a clarinettist

- *Wanted to because*: Like to play, freedom of expression
- *Didn't because*: Couldn't earn enough money, not enough time

4. Learn to fly

- *Wanted to because*: Freedom, mastering new skill, fun, self-indulgence
- *Didn't because*: Never got around to it

5. Master a new language

a *Wanted to because*: Talk to people more when working overseas
- *Didn't because*: Working overseas often, but seven days a week, so no time to learn.

6. Take up mountaineering

- *Wanted to because*: Freedom, exhilaration, natural world
- *Didn't because*: Working too hard, thought I couldn't

7. Develop sensuality

- *Wanted to because*: I want this
- *Didn't because*: I was away working for more than fifty per cent of the year, I was also working weekends when I was away, sometimes at home too, so I didn't see my wife enough.

8. Be financially secure

- *Wanted to because*: Freedom
- *Didn't because*: Don't know, feel bad about it

9. Learn to cook

- *Wanted to because*: Might be fun
- *Didn't because*: No time

10. Get out of business by forty-five

- *Wanted because*: Freedom, see more of family
- *Didn't because*: Came to a career standstill at forty-two and needed to build up finances

This extremely intelligent, analytical man had become so involved in his work that he had eroded his professional and his private tool kits.

He had become highly self-critical. He was very thin, having narrowed his body almost to nothing so that he didn't take too much space in the world.

Looking at his list of ten unachieved ideas it is first interesting to see that freedom comes up several times. He didn't, when he first came to me, believe he could have much of anything else but work and trying to dam up the emergencies of his family life. When he took the time to look at his unachieved ideas he realised just how much he had given up. As well as freedom, he was longing for some fun.

Five months later he was living in balance in a way he had not thought possible. He has started playing the clarinet again, built in holidays with his family and on his own with like-minded friends, was mountaineering, had found the right cookery course and had acquired himself a new job, which paid nearly twice the amount of his old one. When I saw him the last time he was ebullient, 'I really just came back to thank you and show you how much I have gained from all this. I have fun and freedom built in and the new job uses all the strategic skills that weren't flowing in the last one.'

When I asked about the sensuality, he smiled and said, 'That takes a little longer, but I'm on my way.'

STRATEGIC LIFE QUALITIES

Our *strategic life qualities* are the ones we usually don't know too much about, even though they are often the ones that affect us most. They are our hidden drivers, the life qualities that we have had ingrained in us from when we were kids. They come from deep in our past, so deep in some cases, that unless we stop to track them, we don't see the knee-jerk behaviour they drive us to. We need to look for and recognise them in balancing the past and the future because our best-laid plans can be held back by their in-built effect.

One of my strategic life qualities is an urgent need to bolt, to remove myself when hurtful emotional confrontations come up. I have this because of having had a marvellously exotic, but very driven mother who pushed me and pushed me, using her drive, to succeed in everything I did.

I was a teenage ice-skater, competing in Europe and the USA, and I did quite well, but half of why I wanted to skate was to travel abroad, to train in the USA with a group of friends, to be away from the constant pressure. In fact, when I wanted to give up skating, it took me six months to tell my mother, six months of going to the rink every day and working at it, knowing I just wanted to move on and find out what else there might be in the world.

I'm better at it now, I don't bolt at the first sign of emotional difficulty, but I had to recognise it to stop doing it. As a child I used to think, well, if they don't love me I'll go. When I was nine I won a scholarship to my school and my father gave me ten pounds reward money. I went to the local railway station and bought myself a one-way ticket to Paris. I then went into our village and bought a red straw hat. I walked home and announced I was going. My mother was horrified and my father, to his credit, suggested that it wasn't the season for Paris and perhaps I would like to have a tent in our back garden. I lived in this white canvas tent under the pear trees for a year and a half, through two English winters, until one morning I woke to find a family of slugs in my sleeping bag. By then I figured I had staked my independence. I began to ice-skate instead.

I have had to learn that, although this need to bolt or just get away has been more than useful in my work in seventy countries, this ability to set out for anywhere at any time has actually been a priceless gift from my mother. But I have always to be aware that my inclination to bolt isn't too useful a life quality in dealing with the people I love. Away has always been so comfortable for me. I tend to think of it as a safe place. I check into a hotel room and sigh with relief. It is simple, uncluttered.

I have another strategic life quality, just as fundamental, which is that I fight for things I want. It started when I was a kid of five and had chicken pox and was kept in a dark room for six weeks. I remember coming out into the living-room a couple of times, a little kid wanting some hugs, and being told to go back. I felt I wasn't good enough for the life and laughter I saw there. I was in the dark and they were in the golden light of the living-room. I carried for a long time the belief that I wasn't good enough for that light, for the good things in life. Of course it left me with a longing for it. The trouble was that I had to battle, it seemed to little-person me, to get out of my little room at all, so for a long time I battled for the light, for the good things in life, and I didn't know how to just let them happen.

Again, it's a useful strategic life quality to have that kind of metal, it means I do not give up easily. But it isn't a quality that should be at the forefront of my life, I mustn't let it run me – that's too hard. I need to be aware to use it as a strategic life quality when it is appropriate.

DRAWING ON SUCCESS HABITS

When you are looking for the next round of success, it is useful to stop a moment and look at your *success habits*. One of the surprising sides to success habits is that, if left unchecked for too long, they can start to do as much harm as they have previously done good. The danger, as you look back, lies in your thinking you can achieve the future only in the same way as you have successfully achieved the past. Future success, though, often lies in newer, even completely different, territory.

For example, I worked with someone who had been successful for years at turning her own small catering business into several medium-size businesses. Because of this success she was invited onto the boards of several very large companies and institutions. Her main success habit in running her own businesses was that she was always there to inspire people and build teams. When she was in much bigger organisations, she had to drop the habit, which, for instance, saw her dress up in a deep-sea diving outfit at her office Christmas party so that her staff would feel she was one of them. She found this quite difficult at first. Trying to be too close to so many people in the new environment was taking far too much time and taking her away from what she has been hired for in these new board positions. She had to learn to back off and move into a more strategic position.

One of the hardest success habits to break is *doing*. We get through the lower and middle ranks by doing. But as we move up through management, this doing is a drawback. The higher we go, the less we need to be doing. I suggest to clients in this position that they develop a trigger reaction to it. Every time they feel the urge to accomplish something they have to ask themselves if they can get someone else to accomplish it for them.

As you move higher and higher you need to move more and more into concept. Developing and honing the concept ability is what will secure you the success you want, the highest jobs in your company.

To work out what your success habits are, whether you need them any more and which ones you want to change, follow through this process:

- First, make a list of the things you have not done very well in your life.
- Second, make a list of the things you have done very well
- Third, make a list of six things you never want to do again.
- Fourth, list what you want to change.

Make sure you focus on the good stuff rather than the not-so-good stuff. I find too many people like to wallow around in the failures if given a chance. You are looking here for the success habits you want to drop and those you want to carry through into your next success.

A CHALLENGING FUTURE IS YOUR SAFEST PLACE

Each of us carry in our make-up a memory of the earth's history as well as the possibilities for our future. Too often we bury this under day-to-day concerns. It is vital to keep this innate understanding in play. In this way we remain aware that we need to continue to grow and develop at the same time as we change our world and our world changes around us.

A challenging future, one that continues to grow and develop, is the safest place we can put ourselves. Too often, people stay fixed where they are because it is familiar and it appears safer than making a move. What you have to realise is that your body and your mind are designed and built for change, running alongside history's change and the galaxies change and the universe changes.

To fight to stay in one place is moving against the universal energy around you. Unless we use biotechnology and gene power to keep ourselves the same, it is the height of arrogance to think that we and our children and their children and all the generations after us are going to look and behave like us. Why would we think we are any different from a long line of animal and human change?

However, in the context of the decision you make today about your career, if you realise that making changes and moving ahead are actu-ally what is giving you the release of energy you need, that they are your place of power, your safest way of operating, then it becomes eas-ier to make the new career moves.

If you want to attract the most interesting jobs and the most influential people, you need to challenge yourself as much as these people are challenging themselves. Safety isn't a place that goes any-where in business. A solid base, yes, a sure balanced awareness of your footing, yes; but on top of that you need to stretch yourself continu-ally to allow room for new thinking, new achievement and the result-ing successes.

Think about yourself sitting hunched at your desk for a moment. Can you see room in that closed-in body for free-flowing energy, for people to feel you are open enough to attach their new ideas to? Are you open enough, organically and elegantly flowing enough so that everyone around you wants you in their successes?

If you keep trying to accomplish the same pursuits over and over again you wear out the parts of you that are functioning to help you meet these repeated commands. You just use the same nerves or muscles or cells until they give up. Two things happen. The physical parts of you collapse first and then the psychological messages cut in to tell you that you can't do the pursuit any more. Unfortunately, with that psychological message comes the insecurity that says, 'If I can't do that any more, I must be failing.'

When that happens you get fatigued, tired, maybe even exhausted and you start to believe you couldn't start anything new on the ener-gy you have at your disposal.

What you need to do is stop doing all the same things, give those used-up bits of you a rest, and concentrate on challenging yourself in a new area. Allow the dead stuff to fall away and re-invent yourself in your body and mind's newer territory. Starting down a new avenue brings the new release of energy you need. If you try something new and it doesn't give you that release, it is probably too close to what you were doing before.

PART THREE

FINDING THE CENTRE POINT OF YOUR WORLD

This shorter part of the programme lies at the heart of achieving balance. Here you find the central place of comfort that allows you to be your strongest. Here you look at the whole spectrum of your life – through all the layers, from the inner you to the outer you, right through to where you fit in the global picture. Thinking of yourself in this connected way gives you the highest confidence levels and the toughest resilience in any fast-changing situation.

CHAPTER EIGHT

BALANCING THE INNER
AND THE OUTER YOU

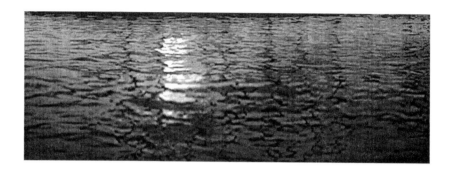

ecognising the difference between your inner and your outer life
helps you maintain balance on a day-to-day basis. Nothing you
could be doing is more important than knowing where the Centre
Point of your life is and being able to connect with it quickly. When you
have it in place you can build solid relationships with all the elements in
your life, from your soul to your company to your nation to your global
interests. In this way you can stretch yourself comfortably to take in the
fullest scope of your life and at the same time stay sturdy, safe and
secure.

FINDING THE CENTRE POINT OF YOUR LIFE

It's a grand thought, finding the *Centre Point* of your life: if we could hold on to this Centre Point we would never get out of balance. How do you find it? When I lose the Centre Point of my world I feel uneasy, as if I don't know where I belong. And sometimes I do lose it; life just gets too busy, or too many people want something from me at the same time, and I lose that secure, solid, safe, pin-point place inside me. I forget that nothing I could be doing is more important than holding on to this feeling.

We tend not to separate the inner and the outer us. We think of ourselves as one functioning human being – 'I'm just me' – which of course we are. But we are more than this one physical entity; we are layer upon layer, starting at our centre with the heart and soul and moving through the rings around our soul to the bigger rings around our lives.

Remember that until you were one year old you took for granted that you were connected to everything around you, you had no sense of separation, you felt safe. But the people around you, for the best of motives, took that safe sense of connection away and you grew to learn that the chair, the bed and your toys were objects that had nothing to do with you. A pity, really, these were hard lessons and you didn't need them, neither were they true. If everything is made up of particles and atoms and other forms of energy, just as you and I are made up of particles and atoms and other forms of energy, then we are all in this together, us and every object we see around us, from grandfather's chair to brightly shining Hale-Bopp comet to fast-moving Porsche.

So, how do you separate the inner you and all these layers of the outer you? More importantly, where do you want to set your boundaries? The illustration opposite shows you in the centre of the relationships you have in the world around you. When you relate to all of these and understand how you relate to them, you will be at your most solid and your most inspirational at the same time.

You can choose, of course, not to relate to all of these rings. You can choose, for example, to function within certain perimeters, say perimeters 1, 2, 3, and 5 (Body, Objects, Relationship and Work), leaving out Soul, Family, Community, Society, Nation, World and

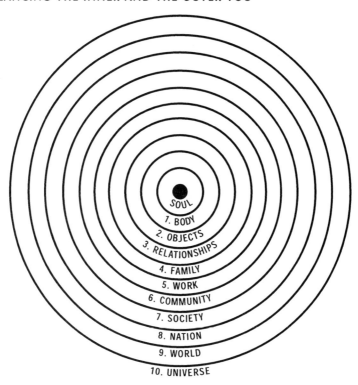

SOUL
1. BODY
2. OBJECTS
3. RELATIONSHIPS
4. FAMILY
5. WORK
6. COMMUNITY
7. SOCIETY
8. NATION
9. WORLD
10. UNIVERSE

Universe, and go along fairly nicely, although perhaps not very inspirationally as we go forward into the millennium, but fairly nicely.

I like to have all the rings in play in my life, the whole one to ten, to be in relationship to all of them as often as I can. For me, this is my safety, the safety of being aware of my relationships to everything from my soul to the cup I touch through to all those stars in the sky which are part of my earliest history.

Sometimes people say at first, 'I don't have time to think about all these relationships, I don't even have time to run my life.' If you choose to ignore your roots and your place on the world and universe you live in, you become an isolated bundle of energy and, therefore, left too often without a secure sense of who you are.

How do you manage this on a day-to-day basis and how do you keep a balance between the inner and outer you? The first step is to develop a very strong inner you. The outer bits are easier to see, and once you have the inner strength sorted out you can cheerfully start to relate to these outer bits more easily. Getting to know more about the inner you, your soul, is a day-to- day affair, sometimes you have a good sense of it and sometimes it goes away, but you have to allow enough quiet time for it to develop and happen. Inside, in that quiet place, you have all the answers you need, the depth of knowledge about what you can be sure you need in your future and how you can balance your inner and outer world.

There are lots of ways to find that Centre Point and there is often far too much fuss about it. Schools of meditation are set up around the world, people in the stricter Zen monasteries force themselves to meditate for hours on a cold floor, those in deep trances in Sri Lanka put hooks through their back. It is much simpler than that. All roads lead to the same thing anyway. Finding your Centre Point is just a matter of checking into the universal quiet and recognising that the bit of you that recognises that universal quiet, the message in your genes, is the very same thing.

We all, instinctively, know the universe has a quiet sound; we see it out there in the skies and we carry it in our body's memory. If we sit on the earth we hear the earth's quiet. We know that we have quiet times in ourselves, we feel them inside us if we sit under a tree, lie on a rock by a waterfall or sit with a bush African listening to the quiet behind the sounds of the bush.

Practically, finding your quiet is just sitting still and listening to your own body's rhythm. Listen to your own breathing, listen to your own heart, allow your mind to slow down, let every muscle and nerve ending in your body come to a complete standstill. Tell your emotions it isn't their broadcasting time. Simply instruct all the functions in your body that it is time to let go for a few minutes. *Do* quiet. There is no mystique about this quiet time; it is the most familiar thing you know, if you just stop and listen to it. It is the innermost place you have and it is your Centre Point.

A useful item to remember is that you can't do quiet when you are *doing* busy. They have to be separated. But, if you *do* quiet for anything from a few minutes to an hour a day, your *doing* busy will be much calmer too.

At the centre of this quiet inside you, when you get to know it better, is a vast pool of universal knowledge, a stream of the same knowledge that is the ongoing force through time. What better way of balancing yourself than checking in with the biggest ongoing balancing act of all?

Once you have recognised the inner you and you have it at your disposal, it is quite simple to build a set of relationships or strategies with all the other rings around your life. Start to think through each of the relationships in the illustration. As you work through each of these and sort out for yourself just where you stand, you will find a greater sense of clarity and ease.

TOOLS

- Sit back in your quiet space and think through the rings in the illustration.

- Take the time to write these out and mark what you might want to change in your thinking to feel more in balance with each of these rings.

- The next layer after your Centre Point and your body is the objects around you. Do you surround yourself with the objects that give you peace or beauty or excitement or inspiration?

- Are your relationships with lovers and friends in a clear state and order?

- Is the family within which you function flowing along as cleanly and lovingly as you would like?

- What do you want your relationship with your community to be?

- What kind of contribution do you want to make to society?

- Is it important to you to play some kind of pro-active role in the life of your nation, however small?

- Is there something you care about in the world arena that you would like to be heard on and if so how are you going to do it?

- How much of a relationship with the universe do you want; is a sense of its energy enough? Do you want to contribute to, say, funding projects that will tell you more about the outer limits; perhaps there are people you would like to meet and be involved with who work at these outer limits?

CHAPTER NINE

BALANCING YOU AND YOUR PLACE IN THE BIGGER PICTURE

F inding what you do most easily that affects the most people puts you in the most effortless place of success. Knowing how you, this one small person, can take a place position, not a title position in your organisation allows you to give most naturally to that organisation. Knowing how you, the individual, fits in the bigger picture, means you operate from a powerful, personal base-level rather than from your more obvious skills.

WHAT DO YOU DO MOST EASILY THAT AFFECTS THE MOST PEOPLE?

One of the mistakes we make in this fast-moving, fast-changing time is to fight constantly for what we want to make happen. There is a lot of talk about goal setting and goal achieving. Because our world is so competitive we often value speed over the extraordinary, planned result over a natural, organic firing. Both ways are useful, of course, but what interests me when I work with my clients is to find out the one thing they do most easily and encourage them to do it. When I ask the question, 'What do you do most easily?' they think I am not asking for anything serious. The first response is often, 'Lie around and read books.'

I go on to explain that what you do most easily is where your inherent power lies. What you fight and strain for costs you too much and brings too much unease, perhaps even exhaustion, into the situation. Then comes stress. Take Peter Jennings, long-time anchor-man extraordinary at ABC television in New York. What does he do most easily? What is it in him that allows him to affect so many people at seven o'clock in the evening, right across the USA?

Set aside his intelligence for a moment, and his ability, long-honed, to make people want to share ideas with him. What is it at his core that he does so naturally that it allows him to function so well in his role?

I first met Peter in Beirut before the war; we went to a briefing on Damascus as preparation before going to Syria the next day. I watched him in Damascus interviewing, probing, building the background he was looking for. What struck me then were two things: first, his gentleness and, second, his constant search for the truth.

When Peter talks to people, whether national leaders or his audience, it is that unthreatening quest for the truth to which they instinctively respond. It is what Peter does most easily, this searching for the truth. It was there in a tiny political attaché's office in the Syrian embassy in Beirut when he was a bright young reporter in the Middle East; it is still there today. What he has added to it over the years is the balance of sophistication and knowledge.

In New York, a few years ago, we talked over dinner, about what he would do if he ever stopped being an anchor-man. 'I'd go back on the road as a reporter. People might think I'm too old, some think I'm too stupid,' he smiles, 'but I still have the fire to do it.' I wouldn't like to see him do that – it is never good for anyone to go back – but it's true; his search for the truth, the power in him, will always give him a place in any picture he chooses to put himself into.

What I do most easily is communicate the new. The first thing I want to do when I see something new is tell someone. I feel good at all stages of this. I like to ask questions about things I do not understand, I feel very excited when I hear the new in the answers, and then I feel quite joyous when I get someone else to understand what I have learnt.

When I was an ice-skater I used to spend far more time on finding a new interpretation of the music than on practising over and over the technical side. I wanted to get the audience to feel the emotions in the music I had chosen. It was a marvellous outlet for a teenager in a private English girls' school. Today, when I get up and talk to groups of people I sometimes feel like the young girl out on that ice, in front of me are all those people to tell what I have been thinking about.

Think back through your current week and see what you did most easily, without using power, adrenaline, coffee or any other driver. Where did you do something so easily that you hardly noticed it and yet it started a chain of free-flowing events?

Then think back to your childhood or your teenage life and see where you were speaking about something when everyone around you agreed with you. See if you can remember the past moment in all its detail, then see where it matches whatever you did most easily this last week. Find the link between that far yesterday and today on this. In that link is the easy way for you to affect the people around you.

TAKING A PLACE POSITION, NOT A TITLE POSITION

When I work with people who are at a career change point I see them trying to fit their skills into the job they are thinking about. I see them rewrite CVs, try to convince employers that the expertise they have is just right for the position. At a time when there are progressively fewer and fewer of the familiar kind of title jobs in large organisations, the belief is that we have to work harder and harder to convince someone to give us one of them.

There is a better way and it is a way that will, first, make you stand out from the crowd and, second, allow you to feel much more confident. When you go into an interview or a discussion on a move within your organisation, take in with you not only the skills you have but also the place position you would like to occupy in the organisation.

First, sort through the way you operate at work and pick out the one thing you are best at, quite likely not one of the skills you were hired to do. You might be the carer in your group, or the negotiator or the one, like Peter Jennings, who has an eye on the truth. Bring this to the front of your thinking and place a very high value on it.

When you think about yourself this way, you are valuing a core part of you, the inner role you play most easily, which will affect people around you. It is your place position. Separating this from the job role, the title position, gives you a double value to your organisation.

If the person hiring you knows you are a good facilitator as well as, say, an achieving sales director, for example, two things happen. First, you put yourself in a position where you can fire most naturally. Second, you also put yourself on an ascending track in the company, which may well be a faster-moving track than competing with all the other eager beavers who want to rise to board level through sales. Sales only goes so far, but a good facilitator with a sales background can make a huge contribution to the functioning of a company's board. Facilitators, at their most sophisticated, make excellent chairpersons.

My daughter, for example, who is twenty-four, has chosen to go into advertising. Her title position, only one year out of university and three salary rises up, is an account manager. Her place position, though, is that she is a natural organiser; she knows inherently how to organise, and the people around her respond to that. Because she organises so naturally and effortlessly, she is the one both fellow employees and clients want to do their work with. She can take this place position into any industry she chooses; it is what will allow her to have several different careers in her lifetime.

Knowing your place position also stops you from moving into the wrong organisations. If the company has a hierarchical culture, and you are a facilitator, then you are not going to be very happy. If a global company, one such as ABB (Asea, Brown Bovery), for instance, has broken into many small, semi-independent divisions, then there are quite a few places for international facilitators.

Along with looking for and communicating the new, I also facilitate the new. I do this all the time; in fact sometimes I have to watch that I don't just do it without noticing in situations where it isn't needed. Give me a group of people, whether three, ten or three hundred, and I bring out the new in them.

When you understand your base-level place position, take it everywhere with you, whether you are talking to friends, family, companies or global organisations. It is almost a careless power, but in any situation you can lead with it if you are fully aware of the power it has.

TOOLS

- Think back through your current week and see what you did most easily, without using power, adrenaline, coffee or any other driver.

- Where did you do something so easily that you hardly noticed it and yet it started a chain of freely flowing events.

- Look for the way you function, not what you actually do, and pick out the personal role you want to take into the next piece of work you do.

PART FOUR

THE BUILDING PROCESS: SETTING IN A STEADY BALANCE

In this fourth and last part of the programme you find the building process for setting in a good balance in your life. Here are the practical techniques which will take you there step by step.

Learn to balance your different life-rhythms, your vision and your commitments. Compare your various financial expectations and draw in your network to help you achieve a solid place of power and higher rewards. Find a new way to negotiating a better balance between your home and your office, re-negotiate your contracts and agreements with your companies. Stand back and restructure the time in your week, your year and your life.

When you have completed this fourth part of the programme you will have all the tools you need, including a quick-reference reminder section in Chapter Fifteen, to begin living your life in balance.

CHAPTER TEN

BALANCING
DIFFERENT RHYTHMS

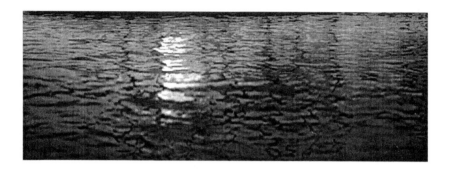

Balancing your different rhythms allows you to choose the way you approach different parts of your life. If you get this right you can slip in and out of the different streams with ease.

Balancing different rhythms means getting the right vision, positioning the vision in your life, making sure your vision isn't mixed up with who you are, and working out how to balance your vision with your existing commitments brings a marvellous sense of relief and freedom.

Here you find out how to start to run a varied, Multi-Channel Life. As you become more aware of the different channels you want to pursue, you can decide where on the globe you want to do each of them.

We are always trying to balance different life-rhythms. When these life-rhythms fall out of gear, when the input gets too much for us to digest, we run out of energy, forget how to laugh and lose a sense of being connected to those around us. We rattle between the components of our lives like goods on a production line that have hit a bottleneck.

I'm often amazed that we balance the contrary rhythms of our lives as well as we do. Even the simplest mixes can be difficult if they are all tangled up. For example, even between couples there are many different speeds. A French television man worked at high speeds all week and needed a Saturday afternoon sleep. His wife was a writer, working at a slower rhythm all week. She wanted to be social on Saturdays, fill the house with friends and new people. They fought over this, thought of it in personal terms, that each one didn't want to share the other's life on a Saturday. This was pretty uncomfortable, one rhythm jostling up against the other.

If you take the personality out of operating differently and think of the other person's inherent life-rhythms, you will find more appreciation. I was married to someone who went at the same fast speed as I did for nineteen years and we wore each other out. If we had understood this about each other perhaps we would have been better at adjusting our speeds.

Take your own life for a moment and work this through; how many different rhythms might you have? You have one rhythm for your children, one with your spouse or partner, another when you are being social. Then there is your vision; at what speed do you want to further that? At what pace you want to set in your fitness? Looking back at your change point, how fast or slow are you going to move through it? And the influences you have so carefully balanced, now that you know what they are, at what rhythm do you want each of them in your life?

Balancing these disparate rhythms, being aware of what they are, is how I keep the different channels of my life in order. Living in a big city, where the pace runs fast around me all the time, I need to consciously switch in and out of different speeds or I would never vary my life, be tempted to run at the same pace as the city around me and then have trouble sleeping easily at night.

Fifty years ago, when big towns were not these giant cities and there wasn't Sunday shopping, late-night shopping, transport running all night and parks full to bursting with people playing radios, running, talking, skate boarding, playing concerts and driving, we had quiet places to go do. Now we don't, it's all full on.

Now, too, getting to a quiet place asks more effort from us; we have to drive long distances, keep operating at a revved up speed. By the time we get to the quiet place we are running too fast and we find it hard to slow. We think we ought to be able to manage all this and feel we are failing when we don't.

We have to learn to play with our possible different rhythms *in situ* so to speak. The Japanese have always known how to do it; when you live in a house or flat with paper walls you learn to respect others rhythms and find your own pace inside you, regardless of the world around you. The Japanese have always known how, for instance, to turn the busy room they live in into a clear, quiet, uncluttered place. They understand how to keep only one object displayed so that their focus on that one object will keep their minds from running and jumping. In South-east Asia and India, where there are altars in the house or in the garden, there is always a place of respectful quiet. Each individual doesn't have to fight for a quiet corner.

With the rise of television and fast communications we have tended to bring into our lives so many different rhythms at once, few of them close to our own. Television takes away the still bit of our life-rhythms, constantly showing us hectic ones. Our respect for what the media offers us has taken a higher rating than our respect for stillness.

With property prices rising and rising, how do we find the still corner we need to slow down, recharge? In our mental pictures of the world we live in we know that somewhere at every moment in the world there is noise, action, purpose, intent, construction, market movement, competition, growth. There are so many rhythms around us that we cannot possibly sort all of them. But they are there, playing away, a background of continuous action we don't know how to deal with.

At what personal speed do you think you operate? If you put a mileage on each of your rhythms, you can get a more tangible sense of them and then decide which ones you want to speed up or slow down.

First, there is your body speed, the way you move, walk, talk and communicate. I think of my speed as fairly steady these days, so I give myself, on a scale of one to a hundred, a nice even fifty-five. This is quite different from my travel writing days when I was probably operating at about a hundred and fifteen, well over a balanced norm of around fifty.

A man I once had a relationship with was a ninety-five mile an hour man. His rhythm was just too fast for me. I always felt I was somewhere just a little behind and I wasn't comfortable. Being with him was a bit like being in a fast sailing-boat with him controlling the rudder; I was off-balance and being thrown around. I was too slow for him and he was too fast for me. In the beginning we didn't notice because we were both running on the adrenaline and endorphins of excitement, but, as time went by, it was obvious to us both that as much as we liked each other as people, we disorientated each other and always would.

When you have your main rhythm in place, think about the other rhythms in your life. How many rhythms do you think you have? Having this awareness puts you in better command of your life. Think of your life for a moment as a Coca-Cola production line. You have hit an operational bottleneck, and your Coca-Cola bottles are jammed still, forcing your production line to stop for a moment. What's happening to the bottles jostling against the narrow point? Mentally put a label on each bottle: for example, *work* sixty miles per hour, *play* ninety miles an hour, *meditation* zero miles an hour, *time with children* twenty miles an hour.

It is useful to be aware of what rhythm you are running at, for example, when you walk in the front door at night. There you are, key poised, body and mind revving at ninety-five miles an hour. Inside, the occupants are on a totally different rhythm. How are you going to deal with this? How could you make it easier for yourself? For them? Stop a moment, check your rhythm. What do you want to change it to for this moment or this next half hour?

If you think about it in this way you will be able to slip in and out of the different streams of your life with ease. Whatever I do, though, however often I change my rhythms, my inner life-rhythm stays the same. These days it is almost like a default on computer, I revert almost automatically to the life-rhythm I need. All of us have this natural life-rhythm that we can revert to. What is yours?

TOOLS

- Think of the different activities of your life in terms of speed.

- Watch yourself for a week or so. Every time you start a different activity, observe how fast or slow you do this.

- Ask people round you where they think you are going too fast or too slow.

- What number would you put on the rhythm you are most comfortable with?

- What number would you put on the rhythm you are most uncomfortable with?

- Which activities do you want to slow down?

- Which activities do you want to speed up?

- If you are out of rhythm with someone important, can you set a new mutual rhythm? Or agree to leave each other alone to do certain activities at your owns speeds?

YOUR VISION AND YOUR COMMITMENTS

You may have a vision and not know how to get it; more likely you don't have a vision at all and wish you did. Perhaps you do not believe in visions but prefer the day-to-day experience of *'I just take life as it comes'*. Maybe you have been successful by plucking opportunities out of the air. 'Luck is in the air,' said Alfred Hitchcock, 'all you have to do is reach out and take it.'

Some of us believe we can't have a vision because we owe it to people around us to look after them. Some don't believe they are worth having one, 'I'm just a housewife, secretary, accountant, a manager'. The worst possibility is to have a heartfelt vision and do nothing about it. People who do this to themselves are usually quite weary or bitter, at the least unhappy.

The woman who came to me, saying that her vision was going to change the life of every woman in Britain is a good example. She had been to a motivational weekend and been raised to these impossible heights. At no time over the weekend had anyone thought to ask her if her vision would balance with her day-to-day commitments. Bob Geldof, of Band-Aid concert fame, is often cited as an example of what one person can achieve if they have a vision. Well, yes, but Bob Geldof's career was at a standstill at this time and he didn't have any other commitments to get in the way of his vision to raise money for Ethiopia, he had all day, every day.

The woman who wanted to change the life of every woman in Britain hadn't actually taken any steps towards her vision. What she needed to do, before embarking on any visionary plan, was to change her own life first, to do for herself what she wanted all the other women to do. I worked with her to bring her vision back to a realistic level, to have this concept for herself. Then she could start encouraging others, within her own life and commitments. Then she would have something reasonable and balanced to take out to others.

Visions are funny things. For so much of my life, since I was five, I had this interior idea that I had come to save the world. Big stuff for a five-year-old, but I used to think my heart would break unless I could save the world. I never quite got rid of the feeling and it held me back.

The feeling came from a bad year I had when I was five. Lots of things went wrong in that year for me but one of the most affecting was probably the time my mother heard about the death of my grandfather on the telephone. We were living in a ramshackle, wooden lakeside house outside Montreal, Canada, with a huge veranda around it, when she got the call. She locked us out of the house – my father, my sister and me – and she howled and howled on her own in her grief.

My child's heart was nearly exploding with my need to help her, to make it better, I can remember it now, but she couldn't allow that, she needed a private grief. As I stood there in the garden I thought my heart was going to break, in a way it did, and I was left with a huge unused need to save people. This grew and grew because it was untamed.

I thought my love wasn't wanted, that what I was wasn't good enough to help her. So, without understanding it at that age, I transferred this need to something more abstract, something of a commensurate size for my need. If I could save the world my heart would get better.

A rather large mission for a little kid, and absolutely out of balance with the rest of my little-kid world. This cross of vision and innocent conceit went subterranean for a long time. I stopped putting the neighbourhood children to bed because somehow I thought I might do them harm, as I thought I must have harmed my mother, for surely that's why she didn't want me close to her when she was hurting so much.

These days I have to laugh at myself. Saving the world, what a message to carry; for something like forty-five years I carried a weight as heavy as Charles Atlas' globe. These days I tell clients who are carrying too much responsibility to imagine a hook on a wall, to walk over to it, and to turn round and hang their worries and visions on the hook.

When I was the travel editor of *Vogue*, people used to ask me why I travelled so much, when I could have commissioned more. 'I don't know,' I used to say, 'I just know I need to see and learn.' My submerged vision was one of the life-strands carrying me from country to country, asking questions, finding out why the interesting people I met were doing what they were doing and how. What was the world about? How did it work? Where were the cross-overs, the associations? Where did the pieces fit from nation to nation?

Was I saving the world at *Vogue*? Of course not, although people used to tell me that when they read my travel pieces they always learned something about life in general as well as the country I happened to be in. I kept moving around the world, seeing more and learning more. But, of course, I was often left with a slightly dissatisfied feeling that I wasn't living up to myself, as if none of it was enough, as if I had failed. How could it not be when my unspoken mission was so vast?

Finally this battle with my vision, this undefined vision, and my day-to-day life, raged so hard inside me that I came to a standstill, not able to move in any direction at all. If I couldn't achieve what my heart wanted, then I wasn't much use was I? My 'real' life suffered. Who was I – the vision or the woman with a husband and child, friends and a job? The fact that I didn't really know what the vision was – because I had effectively buried all of it except for a constant and rather vague feeling – didn't help either. How could I tell anyone that I thought I was here to save the world? They would be quite right in saying I was nuts. So I hoarded my need to help and it hurt not to be able to.

It was only when I understood that it was myself I had to balance that I started to feel more equilibrium. To do this I had to understand that saving the world is something we all, individually, need to do, that saving it is a simple survival instinct we all share in different amounts. Golly, what a relief.

When I saw it this way, I started to see what skills I had that might help this ongoing process. When I had put this bit in place, I could look at my commitments and see which of the things I do all the time I might usefully offer to the survival process.

My commitments right now are keeping my life in balance, generating enough money to be responsible for myself, feeling joy, giving love, receiving love, being a constructive part of the world I live in, helping my daughter to be aware of her possibilities and what she can be in the world. With these comfortably in place I began to understand that my ability to move ahead and learn and change, the things I do every day, anywhere and in many countries, might be helpful to people who were not able to practically develop their visions.

By helping other people to get their visions in proportion to their lives I would certainly be helping change the world, but in the right size and proportion for my skills and my well-being. Ironically, when I got this right, suddenly the media picked me up and started helping me broadcast my ideas and I gained a bigger bit of the world.

With my commitments worked out so clearly I then understood they were non-negotiables, the simple things of life that I wouldn't give up for anyone or anything, any vision, any work or any person. I liked having these non-negotiables, I felt safer.

Until then most of my life had been negotiable, about as far into flexible as it is possible to go. I was a shifting, moving, manoeuvrable, changeable entity. People saw me as wonderfully mobile, excitingly adventurous, a ground-breaker, and they were right; but it was time for me to have some of the safety they took for granted and often moaned about.

These newly understood commitments were pretty easy to balance with my new vision because they were the vision. By bringing my vision into my life, into the centre of it, into the middle of my commitments, how simple I was making my life now.

A client I found difficult but interesting to work with was the opposite of me. He had been stuck for five years, no vision and dedicated to a minimum set of fixed commitments – his wife, his child and his house. For the first two sessions he fought me to stay stuck. I told him that it is pretty difficult to stay stuck when working with me and I could see in his chin that he thought he could best me. I didn't view it as a battle because I know what happens when people are around me; they get a hit of my fast-moving, very strong energy and in spite of themselves they shift along.

'I'm not in debt yet,' he said proudly, not seeing the negative. 'He told me he had earned £6000 in this last year, that he hadn't been able to get a 'proper, full-time job, because of the recession in the early 1990s and my age [forty-eight]'. I reminded him he had been forty-three when all this started to happen. What did he want to do? He didn't have a vision, he told me, didn't know what he wanted to do.

We all care about something, I insisted, we all have something we want to do. It's just that, due to early childhood experiences or early job experiences, we get to believe we can't do it or have it. So we put layers around the idea or feeling or emotion and we can't access it. The longer we don't do what we care about the harder it is to access.

It's too easy a solution to say, as he did, 'My commitments don't allow me to have what I want.' Excuses, excuses, the excuses we build to stop ourselves from having what we want most. I asked him if he owned his house and what it be worth if he sold it, because he had made the point that he had no money but that at least he wasn't in debt. He replied that he would probably get £250,000 after repaying a £30,000 mortgage.

I felt he was taking this home-is-the-hearth commitment too far. How can anyone spend five years being miserable, trying to meet a financial commitment, with a wife in a state of frustration because he couldn't or wouldn't move, when there are so many opportunities and ideas he could take up with all or part of that money? This client was on the opposite end of the vision-versus-commitment spectrum to me. He was subjugating himself to his commitments.

Listening to him reminded me of a funny incident I had in Tonga in the early 1970s with the then prince of Tonga, an extremely tall, gentle Polynesian, now king. We were sitting around at an American peace worker's palm-built home chatting idly about life in the Pacific when the prince picked up a mirror and started to play with the peace worker's kitten. The kitten kept looking in the mirror and then going around to the back to find this other kitten. The prince kept turning the mirror around, so the kitten kept going around the back. We laughed, the kitten didn't know what was real and what wasn't.

In life, in balancing our vision with our commitments, we need always to keep both realities, both sides of ourselves, in perspective, otherwise we react the way the kitten did. We see our vision, but we can't have it because we haven't separated the commitments from the vision. So we go round and round not having what would be easy for us to have.

You do not have to bring in your vision to centre. Achieving a vision can be a separate entity in your life, something you confine to a particular area. Look at your life-balance drawing again. You may want to confine your vision to one box and put a number of only ten per cent on it. For example, your vision may be a short-term one, such as funding and planting trees in a poor neighbourhood. It is something you care about but you are not going to change your life for it.

In the absence of a big vision, perhaps at a time when your commitments are high, say when you have small children, you can still achieve this vision without affecting the family's life. You may even be able to include your family in the vision, so that the time it takes to accomplish doesn't all come out of your personal time but crosses over with time with the kids.

Having a small vision, in a period when your commitments are high and heavy, makes sense. Without adding the stress of overload, you can then enjoy the good feelings that a vision in process gives you and also have the nice, warming heart-success of achieving it.

Getting your vision mixed up with who you are isn't wise. The British woman who died lying in front of a truck carrying live sheep for the Middle East probably made this mistake. She may have thought she was fighting for a vision, which was to gain new legislation to improve the well-being of live sheep being exported from the UK. Actually, this kind of fervour, where the behaviour is out of balance with the point at issue, isn't at all wise. It comes when an individual's need to have a vision isn't acted upon; the need is given to a word-dumb animal. I will fight for that animal, goes the cry, but the drive is redirected from the person's own lack of a vision for themselves. It is fine to fight for sheep, but it is out of balance to die in front of a truck for them, to forget the commitments of the rest of one's life.

A MULTI-CHANNEL LIFE: WHERE ON THE GLOBE DO YOU DO WHAT?

One of the determinants that always amazes me is how people have such narrow definitions of themselves. There is this big, shifting world around them and they see themselves in only one role. I plough through this idea quite cheerfully with them and introduce the idea of a *Multi-Channel Life*.

We are, most of us, heading for what I call a Multi-Channel Life. Instead of being bewildered by the choices we are facing as our work changes around us, why not be one of the early successes in this new way of living? A Multi-Channel Life is the simplest form of operating as we go into the new millennium. To give you a picture of it, imagine one of those early 1940s radios, and see yourself switching in and out of the different channels of your life as easily as turning the radio's dial.

First, you need to untangle your life until you can see each channel clearly. Then spend some time arranging them in the form you choose; again it's a bit like radio bandwidth, but here you can choose what the broadcasting frequency is. This way of thinking gives you the facility to play different roles at different times in different places with different people. It means that if one of these channels falls out of play, you have several others already engaged.

For example, if you are made redundant, you already are developing or have developed other channels you can pick up, so you can view the redundancy cheque as a bonus to use as you move through the transition stage, not a life-line. You have only had one channel turned off, the rest are still broadcasting. I so often see people who have run along in the same one-channel rut and are then resentful when someone takes that rut away from them

And if you decide you want a Multi-Channel Life, where on the globe do you want to do what? How can you stretch the form to include the widest variety of what you are interested in? A good example of this is an enterprising man in Melbourne, Australia, called Steve Howard. Steve started up a global virtual business. He also started a global foundation so that his private interests were met. He works the two together; on the back of the foundation he builds commercial contacts and furthers his global business, on the back of his business he furthers the issues he is passionate about. He has worked in both the voluntary and the private sector and he understands that both function better for being well linked.

Steve sat back and planned this cross-over of private interests and business gain. He wanted business contacts in the USA so he engineered, through his own foundation, the setting up of a Centre for Australian and New Zealand Studies at Georgetown University, Washington, breeding ground to such powerful alumni as President Bill Clinton. He needed solid links with Japan and South-east Asia, so he set up a branch of New York's very prestigious Asia Society in Melbourne and a media-exchange with the Australia–Malaysia Society. The UK and Europe were also important, both for business and pleasure, so he master-minded an Australia–European Dialogue.

All this manoeuvring took him three years, but he then had collaboration with major corporates and leaders in each of the countries in which he wanted to work and play. His answer to 'where on the globe do you do what?' was to interlock the three places he liked, Asia Pacific, the UK, and the American East Coast to three different but interlocking business ventures at any one time.

Slightly less complicated but just as rewarding is the concept of linking business-to-pleasure-to-learning-to-family, rather than separating them. In this context, 'Where on the globe do you do what?' works like this. I recommended to a much-travelling client doing business in Japan to start by taking up a Japanese martial art, or calligraphy, or learning to grow a Japanese garden, both at home and during his business trips. This would be good for business links, in conversation and in interest shown; visiting the gardens in Japan would be instructive *and* relaxing; and these pursuits would also be good for his health.

He also could involve his family if they all agreed to develop the new skill together. They would feel less left out of a possibly threatening unknown. As he progressed the business, he could also progress his family's involvement. He would be putting himself in a stronger position *vis-a-vis* his work and be less isolated from his family. These possibilities are obviously more manageable than starting Steve Howard's global business, but they may also lead to something just as big when contacts and possibilities come through new and nicely balanced channels.

Structuring a Multi-Channel Life is fairly simple. The first point to realise is that you can start the first steps of this way of living and working today, regardless of how you have been running your biography.

When people come to my *Life Strategies* or *Life Balance* lectures I tell them they should either commit to doing one new thing within twelve hours or leave now. The future starts now, I say, it doesn't start next week or next year. This usually produces a silence. No one has left yet but I wouldn't mind if they did; better to leave right then and go home, than do nothing and feel bad about it.

There is a really simple, no-cost way to start yourself figuring out what you want in your Multi-Channel Life and where on the globe you are going to do what. The exercise works in two stages.

Stage One

- First, you make a list of the possible channels you might want in it, probably not more than seven possibilities. Then you get seven pieces of paper big enough to stand on and write the name of each of the channels on one of the pieces of paper. So there you are, sitting at your desk, a serious person, and I'm going to ask you to get up and play a little game with yourself.

- Spread the pieces of paper around the floor. Walk over to each piece of paper, one at a time, and stand there for one minute. What you are doing is seeing what it feels like if you stand in the middle of your channel or possibility.

- You may feel a little foolish as you lay out the pieces of paper but the exercise works. It is something to do with putting yourself an a situation where you are standing, focused, on these islands of your choice.

- Which of these possibilities feels most comfortable? Which papers do you want to stay on and which feel cold or uncomfortable? You will be surprised at how strongly you do react to standing on bits of paper. This is an intuitive game so it's feelings you are after, not the workings of your intellect.

Stage Two

- Repeat this private game again, but put the names of the places where you think you might want to achieve each of the channels you felt comfortable with in stage one. I don't mind if you are laughing by now, a bit of laughter might be useful anyway; it helps to be relaxed when you are hopping around like a mad person from country to country, both in this exercise and in reality.

CHAPTER ELEVEN

BALANCING YOUR FINANCIAL EXPECTATIONS

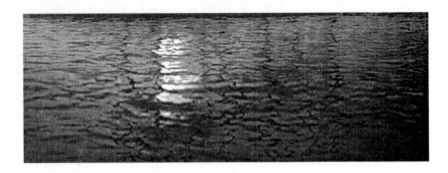

With the new communications technology leading towards a totally flexible and transparent international financial and banking market, our own financial equations are changing from day to day. We can place our money anywhere we want and we can earn it in several places at one time.

In this climate the financial equations in your life need much more attention. Here you look at the pragmatic issues – where do you want to spend what? What are the newer directions that will bring higher rewards? How are you going to earn longer? Not having a lot of spare money isn't a barrier to change. To be optimally financially successful you have to keep in mind a balanced picture of where you want to spend what in order to get the revenues you want.

WHERE DO YOU WANT TO SPEND WHAT?

Because people often see money as a barrier to making a change or getting what they want – 'I can't change, I can't afford it' – they choose
to think of the sum of money they have as finite and portion it out to
their various commitment in their lives, with just enough left over for
the future.

When I ask, 'Where do you want to spend what?' they tend to smile
at me ruefully and say they would like a better house or a more glam-
orous car or something else that they currently cannot afford. In other
words, they put themselves in a wanting position before they think
through what a new and bigger lump sum might be that would allow
them to start deciding where to spend what.

Because they have not stopped to see where a bigger lump sum is
going to come from, they think it will come only by doing more of
what they already do. And, since doing more of what they already do
would be too demanding and stressful, they decide to do without, wait
for ten years or hope for the lottery. This is because most of us carry a
belief-system that says that is how money comes to us in the world we
know, by doing more of what we already do.

Too many of us carry another belief-system that is equally bruising
– that there isn't enough money in the world to go around. It is true
that there is a finite amount of money on the globe at any one time,
on any particular day. Take any day of the year and there is a certain
amount of money moving around on our little ball of earth.

But there are no rules set down anywhere, by anybody, that say
where that money is to be distributed; this distribution isn't a law of
the universe. Who says where it is to go? Who decides who is going to
have the best chunks at any given moment? If you think about it sensibly you'll know that no one decides this; it's up to all of us to decide
for ourselves.

If you look at who has what and when they have it, it proves my
point. Bill Gates has had the biggest individual lump sum for five or
so years, before that someone else had it. The Fortune 500 had
$11,434.8 billion in revenues between them in the year 1995–96, and
what decided the top five positions in this five hundred was the ability of companies such as General Motors, Ford Motor, Mitsui,
Mitsubishi and Itochu to build success in the eyes of all their con-

stituencies, that is, their stockholders, employees, consumers, suppliers and communities.

Within these top five companies, it is the ability of the individuals at the top to keep in mind a balanced picture on where they want to spend what to get the revenues they want. That is what we pay them those huge amounts of money for, to be aware constantly of the whole scheme of things. It's a skill, like any other, but they have concentrated on it a great deal during their lives.

You need to think the same way. To help you start, draw yourself a plan in colour with all the elements you want to spend money on in your life, the whole gamut of them, from eating more expensive organic food to climbing Mount Everest. Get them all down. Have fun with this, do it with laughter, not with longing or despair. Use colour so that the picture takes on a life of its own, so that it jumps off the page at you and demands attention in your busy mind and finds a place in your heart.

We sometimes want too many things at once and this gives us first the feeling, and then the ensuing truth, that we can't have any of them. Wanting too many things is a very effective breaking system. Look at your colourful picture again. Are there too many wants? Do you need to take a few out? Do you need to clarify the picture until it shines a little clearer? When you think you have the level of wants right, colour it again, using plenty of yellow – yellow, like the sun, is the colour of happiness and power.

Looks good doesn't it? The only thing now stopping you from having the money you want to spend are the belief-systems that run you. It was nothing to do with your education, or your background, or your environment, these are all easy blames. The person who decides what share of that many trillion global pot you have to spend is you. I could name many examples of people who have made money who come from as many different circumstances as it is possible to describe. You know them all, but you probably think of them as exceptions.

What you need to remember is that we are all absolutely individual, that is something we do know about ourselves. Each of us has that fingerprint, that life-print, a set of DNAs and a collection of emotional, intellectual experiences that make us unlike anyone else. So, if you are an exception in any way, why not a financial exception? The only thing stopping you from being one of these many financial exceptions is a horribly vague, undefined mindset.

You may think that because you vote in and pay politicians to solve the country's money issues that your responsibility stops there, that you are outside the bigger financial responsibilities. You probably think that in your busy day-to-day life you do not have time to think about all those financial issues that fill the money and financial sections of all the newspapers and magazines.

This is true, if you try to keep up with the sum of the total shifting, changing financial picture. But if you pay attention to the *concept* of the shifting, fast-changing picture, that's your entry point. If the picture is as shifting and changing as fast as this, isn't this the proof that in the middle of all these constant mutations, there are many, many places for you to place your bid, many, many places for another possibility – yours?

If you use the new technologies, everything you need to know to find yourself that niche is sitting there on the web/internet. All you have to do is apply a lively mind and a determination to find that niche. If you don't use communications technology then I suggest you go out and take a course tomorrow. The communications industry is the second money-earning industry on our planet. It is not going away and it is not going to slow down. You can no longer sensibly try to attract money or expand your income without it.

Increasingly it is going to be where money is going to be made and spent. If where you want to make or spend your money is in Outer Mongolia, Taiwan or Australia and you live in Boston, you aren't going to do it by counting your pennies in the family bank. Technology gives you the global financial reach of any of the international, transnational or global companies, it's just your niche that is smaller.

And money isn't like the environment; by making and using more of it we don't deplete our world. By making and using more of it we have the opportunity to improve our lives and the lives of people around us.

A woman in Los Angeles, who runs an arts foundation and writes novels, loves what she does but doesn't make enough money. I suggested to her that she was overdoing it on the familiar creative side of her life. 'But I don't want to be like one of those people who only thinks about money.' 'Fine,' I said, 'but how much time do you actually give to making money?'

She was confused for a moment and at first answered. 'Almost none.' I queried this. 'Well, I guess all the time I am writing or what-ever it is I am putting energy into goes towards making money.' I asked for more time that she could think of. 'What about the time you are thinking about not having enough, what does that add up to?' She laughed.

How much time do you spend thinking or worrying every day about not having enough money? How about rescheduling this time into dealing with money matters? How about cancelling one of your fashion, housing or boating magazines and buying a money mag and reading it in the time you usually moan? How would you feel at the end of the week if that moaning time had actually turned into an new avenue for making money, which both stimulates your mind because it was new territory and gives you the new cash flow you need. Nice thought, when you toast your creativity with a glass of champagne on a Friday night, that you can afford Krug, not just Napa Valley, that you can spend some of it on one of the good causes you want to care about.

BALANCING EXISTING AND NEW FINANCIAL NEEDS

This is the straightforward, practical part of balancing your financial expectations. Getting the financial equation right on an ongoing basis requires you to work on it every day, just as you work on your job every day and just as you put in your quiet time every day. You need to open up your Excel or Lotus sheets every day and see how the day's events affect what you have been doing and what you need to do in your future financial arena. By every day I do not include the weekend or your days off; nothing works well if you continually throw yourself at it.

In these financial areas of your life you notice I am bringing in the technology avenue. We all know how to work out a creative new busi-ness idea on the back of an envelope, but to find the time to build and maintain a business plan or your own growing finances in our demanding times requires technology. Working with this speed and access is a must if you are to build new future expectations into your current situation.

With all the numbers crunched out in front of you, you have a solid base for the unexpected to fall into. We try out *what if*s in a company situation, for a new venture or a new market, but we rarely apply *what* *if*s in this practical way to our own lives.

A good example of doing this was a client I worked with whose stock options in a small technology company gave him the sort of small fortune of which he would never have dreamed. He had projected his small fortune's earnings into the year 2040, still keeping himself in the same framework within which he lived, so it was a very limiting exercise. I asked to him to open up the Excel package on his computer, break the sum up into all kinds of sizes and apply what ifs to each of them.

He had a very good analytical mind so he went at the job with plenty of interest. He worked at it for half an hour a day (he was still in the company) and after a month, he started to see he could live in the country, buy a share in a plane, start part-time on projects he was still interested in achieving for his company and in a few years perhaps start an environmentally sound gardening centre in California.

The power of technology-based, fast *what if*s in opening up our possibilities and bringing us a new balance between past and future expectations is exponential, and the sooner you understand this the sooner your futures are going to look vastly better than your present. Using technology is the same as having several consultants and several international financial journalists in your living-room at the same time, only much cheaper.

By using technology, too, we can see if our future wants and needs have a reality. Because these needs are in the future it is easy to think we will get to them some day, without ever actually setting in the steps to get there, and the result is often disappointment or a sense of failure. Find out today whether what you want is realistic tomorrow, not tomorrow when you come to have a go at it.

If you are looking at a possibility you want to invest in, look at the future today:

- First, ask what is your money going to be worth at the given date in several different fields, including leaving it dully in your bank?

- Second, what is the money you want to invest in this particular object or venture going to be worth on the same date?

- Third, and more important, look at the sum of money you are promised for the investment in the future and work it back to see what that sum would be worth today in real terms, allowing for lost interest and/or opportunity cost. This is the step so few people take the time to work out. When they do, they are often shocked to see that the present value of this future cash flow generated from the investment is not what they would expect it to be.

- Use your technology to know these answers and if the equations don't match, then this idea of yours, or someone else's, doesn't provide a good balance between today and tomorrow.

- Compute the way you have been running your finances and project them into the future, so that you can see what you will have in ten, twenty or thirty years if you go on the same way. Is that satisfying to you?

- Now compare your computed past and your future financial expectations. When you have both sets in front of you, the ways in which you need to change become very clear.

NEW DIRECTIONS BRING HIGHER REWARDS

'I could balance my life better if I had more money,' I hear, or 'I can't change to a job that would make my life easier, I can't afford it.' I always smile when I hear these self-imposed barriers to entry.

Stop for a moment and think of yourself as a company going into a new market. You are the company and the new market is the place you want to enter, a place of financial ease. If your product was having a little difficulty going into a new market, would you accept that? Wouldn't you get the marketing, strategy and sales teams together and decide what the next moves are? Might you decide that the product needed tweaking a little? Certainly you would need to create a public perception of what you were launching.

We hold our financial worries to ourselves thinking it's not very attractive or it is showing failure if we tell others. It's true that you do not want to go around saying to people, 'I don't have any money,' or 'I don't have enough money.' Apart from the fact that this is boring conversation, it's not very confidence boosting for you, nor will it inspire confidence. So, how do you find the newer direction that brings you the higher financial rewards?

You are always worth the sum of all your experiences in life. It is merely a question of how you put them together so that you move into a new field with all the accumulated confidence of what you have done and learned. How do you put a price or a demand on that? By knowing that it is your wisdom you sell, whatever you age. The wisdom you understand you have, whatever age you are, has a much higher value than what you do all day in any commercial situation.

If you can see the way of things, the concept needed to find a way ahead, the Centre Point in any situation, you will be the person others will want to pay money to. That is your value, the wisdom you have achieved. This wisdom can be used in any company, any charity, any institution.

The newer the direction the more likely you are to be able to sing out your insight. You come to it with a clean mind and fresh understandings. Standing back, going through this process of balancing your life and being aware of all the pieces in it, from financial expectations to the rings around your soul, will help you to up-value your contribution to the world around you.

LONGER-TERM EXPECTATIONS: EARNING WHEN YOU ARE EIGHTY

However carefully we predict into the future, we have to accept that it is a fluid place. I find in my classrooms in business schools that participants in their thirties are already worried that their pensions are not going to be enough, and they are probably right. We are looking at living longer, so we are looking at earning longer.

People come to me in their fifties and sixties saying that they are about to retire and they have no idea what to do. If you are thirty, it isn't easy to imagine yourself in your seventies and eighties. In my twenties and early thirties I always used to say I would be quite happy to die at fifty, I would have done all I wanted by then. I'm glad that wasn't one of those self-fulfilling prophecies that motivation people talk about as being the sure way of getting what I wanted and that I'm still here. I have, though, been thinking, since I arrived at that artificial cut-off point, what I would be doing in my eighties.

It has to be something different or I will be bored, so it may be something I don't know about or hardly know about now – after all, this is thirty-plus years away. It has to be something I will make money from, so that I can ensure an income, in case one of my current incomes fail. I need to be able to progress at it. As I will be in my eighties it should be something that will keep me healthy. It also has to make me feel that I am both contributing something and still connected to the world around me.

Of course my eighties income earning doesn't have to be only one thing – on my track record it is unlikely to be – I shall probably still be writing one day a week and speaking one day every two weeks. But as I looked at the criteria I set, I could see that the most likely new way I'm going to earn money then is by teaching yoga. Teaching yoga fulfils all my criteria, and what a nice way to go out of the world, standing on my head!

Set your list of criteria in the same way and see just what your options might be. That tired old word, retire, is probably best expunged from your vocabulary, right now. You may want or need quite seriously to start something tomorrow so that you can be earning from it in fifty or thirty years, or ten.

Perhaps it is appropriate at this point to have a look at your field of ideas from Chapters Two and Five again. Sitting somewhere on those blades of grass are the very ideas you need to slot in to earn in your eighties. In Chapter Fourteen: Balancing Your Time, I will look at how to restructure your now and tomorrow so that you can start to add these futures into your life.

CHAPTER TWELVE

BALANCING YOUR NETWORK

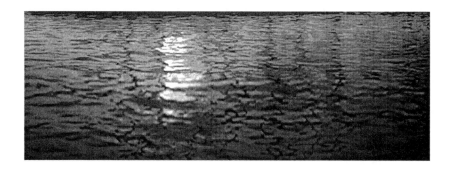

I t is time to look around and see where the support is. When you have the right support to move forwards, you are at your strongest. It is also time to lose the fear that stops you from exposing to the world around you what it is you really, really want to do.

WHAT WILL EVERYONE AROUND YOU HELP YOU TO DO?

There is still an overhanging philosophy from the 1970s and 80s, the 'me time', that says we must not do what others want us to do or we will lose ourselves, lose our particular identity. I want you to turn this upside down and start to think along the lines of 'What will everyone around me help me to do?'

I see many clients who hold on, inside, to some part of themselves they don't want to expose to the world around them for fear of being taken over or for fear of being told they cannot have it. Far better, they think, to hold this part of themselves safe inside than to see it trampled over or find that they cannot have it.

Why should you lose yourself if you do what others want you to do? Is it that you think the collective intuition around you is out of sync with you? Do you really believe everyone around you wants the worse for you? Is it that you don't trust the world around you enough? Or are you so used to making your decisions on your own to ensure you get at least some of what you want that you are actually not in balance with the people around you?

The place of support you have when everyone around you wants to help you is where another large shot of your power and your strength lies. When you are in balance with the network of people around you, it is the most liberating feeling; the playing field at your disposal is very large.

Think back to Chapter Eight on the inner and the outer you for a moment; what you are doing if you look for this place of support is planting the network around you that enables you to move through all the rings around your life. What you are adding is all the helpful and skilled people you know to help you function from a place of connectivity.

The people around you often have very sound ideas on what your next step might be. An Australian man is the perfect example. For many years he dutifully and successfully filled his role as partner in a small business, rebelling inside all the while, but never allowing himself to move away. His father had been dutiful too; after the Second World War men in Australia stuck to their jobs and brought up their families, this was the *fair dinkum* straight and narrow. And this man duplicated his father's behaviour.

His friends watched him and saw his butterfly nature trying to get out. Fortunately for him, they saw it as his actual strength, not his weakness, as he had seen it. Encouraged by them and their offers to take up new roles in several new fields, including an influential voluntary position in the arts, he finally broke away from his constraints.

Now his friends come to him with ideas all the time and these days he listens to them very openly. As a result he has varied roles in the arts, sports, business and global civic futures; he is, for example, producing a film. He has now expanded his network around the world. He can hardly believe his luck. 'It took a very good friend to offer me the first opportunity. At that time I hardly even knew it was close to my heart, what I wanted was so buried. At first I felt I ought not to be so scattered, that I should stay much more focused, but now I love all this diversity.'

BUILDING THE NEW NETWORK

The Australian man was lucky, his friends kicked him along and he had the grace to go with them, even though, initially he wasn't sure. If you are not at the point where your friends are doing this for you, then start the process yourself.

When I worked in this way with George Bain, trawling through lists of his friends and business acquaintances, he changed the place he had thought he would live when he finished full-time academic posts. As the *Financial Times* put it, 'His reflections with Farwagi will disappoint Vancouver real estate agents but bring a flutter of anticipation to the hearts of these who sell land an hour's drive form Winnipeg.' Said Bain, 'I always assumed that in time I'd spend a quarter of my year in Canada. The more we chatted about this aspect, though, the more I realised that a lot of the resources I'll need, a lot of the best networks for me are not on the western seaboard, which I got to know in navy days and where I thought I d end up, but in the Prairies.'

Start to look at your network in this different way. Here is a three-stage process to help you rethink the people around you and rethink what you might want to do with them and what they might want to do with you. You will be surprised at the new avenues and opportunities this process opens up.

First Stage

List all your friends and acquaintances under the categories they fall into, for example, banking, making a difference, venture capital, small business, outdoor life. When you do this you will be surprised at where you will list some of them. A person you have known for years in one role may well come up in another role. Some may come up under several roles, which is fine. Think right back to your teenage days, your university friends and then through your adult life. You should have in the region of seven to twelve categories. This part of the process helps you to reassess the people around you and your relationship to them.

Second Stage

Draw a network like the one pictured. Put yourself in the middle and slot in your friends and acquaintances at the proximity or distance that you now see them. When you have them there, think about the traffic between you and them as two way. What would you want to do with each of them? What might each of them want to do with you?

Third Stage

Redraw the network, as overleaf. Fill in the first lines of the network with the qualities you want closest to you now. You can see from the illustration below that this person wants people close by who are clear, supportive, quiet, prosperous and gentle. Choose your own words and put them in. Fill in the second line of the network with the kinds of activities you want to be doing. In this network the choices are being involved with a cause, being by the sea, being by some woods, having plenty of space, working with an influential, international group of people.

On the outer ring, fill in the precise places and people you want to be doing these things with. Here you see Australia, England, West Coast America. There are also two corners left open, with question marks. This was because the person knew she wanted to develop a bigger place network but wanted to leave that until she had the rest of it firmly in place, up and running.

This network is now the visual for how you are going to keep in balance with the people around you and the roles you develop with each other. It is also a clear visual for the qualities you want in your life at this stage. Keep checking in with it. If too much has intruded that doesn't fit the network, call yourself in on the intrusions and see where you have lost the balance you wanted.

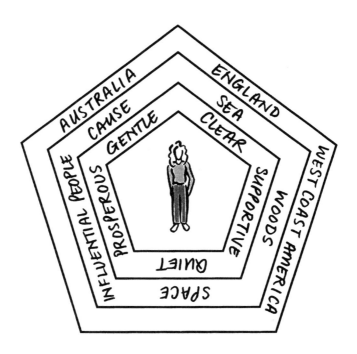

CHAPTER THIRTEEN

BALANCING HOME AND OFFICE

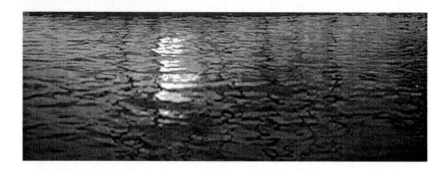

I n this fast-changing business picture you need to learn to balance
your home and office life more than ever before. In the 1990s we have
all become more aware of our individual needs. The next step is to
negotiate these so that our families and our companies want them for
us too.

If you want successfully to combine a high level of personal fulfilment
with ambitious career mastery, you have two crystal-clear responsibilities. The first responsibility is to be so resoundingly clear on what you
want that your case is irresistible. The second is to know how to negotiate this with your family and office so that they want it for you too. In
this chapter you learn the secrets of getting heard, as well as a useful,
simple way of discussing a serious life-topic called Clean Listening.

HOW WOULD YOU LIKE IT TO BE?

The first step in balancing home and office is to sit down and think about how you would like it to be. Get a piece of paper and draw out your week, including everything you want in it. The interesting thing about the human mind is that although we say, 'Oh, wouldn't it be wonderful to do nothing,' almost no one will leave the week empty when they do this. While we long to do nothing at times, when actually faced with nothing we tend to fill it up.

Part of this is habit, part of it guilt. As one of my British stock exchange clients said to me, 'One couldn't be doing nothing, one would be thought a dilettante.' Doing some nothing, some real nothing, is good for all of us. Having some nothing time, every week, is very restorative. Nothing time is when we clear our heads so that we can allow in new behaviours. It is also time when we are not playing any of the roles we have agreed to take on. It helps us to balance home and office, because it is neither.

The first action to take in balancing home and office is to introduce some other ongoing main action so that you don't think of your life as divided between home and office.

A man I met about ten years ago had became so stuck in this rat run, home to office, office to home, that he couldn't see any alternatives. In panic he went to a motivational weekend, got struck by the weight of his life and suddenly felt he had to change, fast. He was going to leave his family, leave his job of ten years, buy a sailing boat and sail around the world. When I met him he had sailed around the world and had a good time. The only problem was that he hadn't seen his wife and kids for a year and they were deeply angry with him and he had no idea of what to do next. His finances were low and he wasn't feeling too self-confident. Companies aren't too wild about people who just disappear and he was having trouble finding work.

If he had stopped to think his life through, done some strategic planning, he could have done all the things he wanted to do, perhaps over a longer time, and still have had something to come back to.

One of my clients came to a similar point in his life. He wanted to sail around the world, too. We did the strategic planning. We gave quite a bit of time to looking first at what everyone else around him wanted to do, at home and at the office. Once he had this information we drew it all out on a huge piece of art paper. We had everyone else's life and needs clear, so when we planned the track for him to take so that he could go sailing, he could be considerate of home and office and still plan in his sailing.

We divided the sailing into four three-month segments and negotiated three months every three years with his company, so that over twelve years he will have done what he had wanted. He didn't initially think his company would buy this, but when he offered to come up with some defined new creative strategies for the job and the department he would be coming back to after each time he was away, they said yes.

He was able to negotiate with his family too. He, too, has a wife and two children. They would all sail with him for two weeks of each segment, then one would sail with him on their own for two weeks. In this way he built in some marvellous time with each of his children and his wife as well as time on his own. He planned sailing courses for himself over the first three years, and studied everything he could about yachting, including navigating by the stars, so that when the first three-month period came up, he was well prepared.

All of this planning and activity gave him another stream to his life that wasn't just office and home. It was something progressive, so it gave his life another ongoing purpose. He had time to himself, some out-there-in-the-middle-of-nowhere nothing time, which gave him a very useful chance to clear his mind.

This fresh approach has lead to a new perspective on his company's activities and both he and his company developed a new alliance in the process. He gained a new, very strong alliance and appreciation of his family as well, becoming more aware of what each side wanted from each other.

Having another thread to his life that was as ongoing as home and office gives him a much sturdier sense of balance. He no longer feels he is leaving himself out.

NEGOTIATING YOUR NEW POSITION WITH FAMILY AND OFFICE

The director of human resources, central staff, at Levi Strauss, has some very positive and useful suggestions about negotiating something you want with your office:

> When someone comes to me with an individual scheme, and I get about one a month, I ask them to put down a written proposal. I help them understand how to phrase it so that their particular manager can see it and I talk to the manager about what the benefits would be for him. I also suggest that this person might offer to take on a job that no one else wants. I have to say, though, that the people who usually get a yes on their idea are the ones who show they are way out ahead. The ones who are receivers would have to do a lot to change their attitude to get this kind of leeway. Also in this changing business climate we would be looking at projects with a shorter life.

I had to learn to negotiate this way quite young. As an ice-skater in full-time school I wanted time off to train. There was no precedent for this in the late 1950s and early 60s, at that time in England you did these sporting pursuits in your spare time.

The first time I went in to talk about this with my headmistress I was eleven. I had told my mother I would handle it and with knocking knees and non-regulation shoes I did. Against quite fearsome opposition I garnered myself an initial five hours off school a week. In fact, I became so adept at it that I remember the tall, ceremonious, silver-haired Miss Connolly saying to me when I was about fifteen, 'Tell me, Peta Lyn, how much of you are we going to see this term?'

The negotiation was a step-by-step process, over a period of years. I knew that was the best way, even at that young age; I also understood that if I promised good exam results this would be good for the school and, therefore, help my case. I was a scholarship winner at the age of nine, and my headmistress feared I would ignore school if I spent too much time on the rink.

I failed Miss Connolly once, when I was thirteen, under-performing in my exams, and she hauled me in. 'You made a commitment,' she said starkly, 'to do well in your exams. If you break our pact, skating goes.' I thought quickly. What else could I offer? 'I promise to bring my marks back up,' I rushed, 'and I think I could work harder at throwing the discus, so I could represent the school at the District and County sports.' How could she resist?! Perhaps I was a precocious youngster, but we all got something we wanted.

Another client wanted to do more mountain trekking, 'But I can't. By the time I holiday with my wife and small kids there isn't any time left.' We plotted several years ahead for him, too. His human resources people were less willing at first and we had to think harder about reasons they would benefit. When he told them he would be prepared to set aside five weekends each year to take other executives on team-building trekking, they agreed to his extra time off.

By putting up a clear schedule of mutual benefit he gained company support. He also became better friends with the other managers he took with him, had even more time on a mountain for himself and gained a new, continuing level of fitness. He was also doing something with his company other than his job, strengthening his alliance with them, so that he became a more integral player. The company gained some free team-building for its executives, which for them balanced out financially the time he was away.

It is very rare for a company or a spouse to be cross because of some inspiring personal success. They are cross, usually, because they do not feel part of it. What you have to do is take these people along with you. Knowing what their plans are, looking at what they need from you and satisfying that in the best way you know how, will help you to carry them along in your new pursuit.

Also, if you are clear on what you want to do, and give the people around you detailed information about it, which you keep up to date, they will not be frightened that you are neglecting them. The hardest part about taking time away from people you love who want you to be with them is dealing with their fear that they will be unloved or unwanted. Keep them informed, perhaps give them some kind of role in the new venture and you take away that fear.

There are many long-held myths about our relationships with our companies. One of the strongest is that when we make an agreement or we sign a contract we believe that what is written there is fixed for the term of our employment. Not so. You can re-negotiate any contract, at any time it becomes necessary. If your company wants to promote you, they can choose to do that. If they want to retrench you, they can do that. So, it follows logically that if you want to promote yourself, you can also find a way that isn't written in the contract.

People I talk to who are management consultants are very sensible about this; they usually hire an employment lawyer when signing any kind of employment contract. When they want to change it, they get that lawyer in again to help them re-negotiate the contract.

Most companies are more flexible than their employees think, but you do have to educate them. They are corporations and institutions, and they have been behaving like corporations and institutions for a long time and have to be encouraged and helped to think in new ways. If you want something different, it is your responsibility to find a way through to that something different. This is your life and this is your company. It is up to you to make the traffic here equal.

It is up to you to work out your new position, the way you want your role to be and re-negotiate it with your company. If we are all evolutionary beings then we are at our best when we are evolving, so you might as well keep strong and powerful by doing just that, developing an evolving role between you and your company.

An extremely bright young woman in her thirties at Microsoft has done just this, although, until we talked, I think she hadn't quite measured just how successful she had been; she was still seeing the struggle. Having succeeded in building a quietly successful career by continuously re-negotiating her position, she is a treat to talk to. Softly spoken, attractive, with a noticeable inner quietness that comes both from her yoga/meditation and her place on the leading edge of one of the world's most visionary companies, she shines with the clarity and confidence she has developed through making this all work.

In this young woman's first year in the company she worked workaholic days twice a week. 'You stayed there until you all met the goal, often till early in the morning. The first two years I remember working seven days a week.' There was always both the lure of the stock options and the high of being at the leading edge of the market, and in the early stages this sustained her through the stress.

When she decided to have her first child and wanted to work only ten hours a day she had to prove that she could still deliver the goals. Staring at her was demotion to a less creative group and less stock options and she wanted promotion. 'We are supposed to have flexible hours, but what it really means is that we are flexible to do more hours than people in other companies.'

She started to negotiate a new structure of working for herself, starting at ten and finishing at eight, but that was not enough for either the company, or her child and husband. There is supposed to be child day-care support but, big issue though it is in every company meeting, it doesn't happen. She tried several time-structures, including starting very early in the morning so she could finish in the afternoon to see what had become her three children over the next few years, but she couldn't get away.

Her best way of balancing work and her family is to bunker down at work and produce. She doesn't socialise there, although she realises that is a disadvantage, but it is the only way she can get through the amount of work on her plate, not fail and get the promotions. She took up yoga and meditation to balance the intensity of the pressure to succeed and that works for her. She meditates at least thirty minutes a day and does two ninety-minute yoga classes a week. 'This has allowed me to become focused and relaxed.'

Her re-negotiating process has been gradual and informal. All the way along, she proved, first, she could do the work, and on that basis, moved toward getting more time for herself and her family. With each boss, she has had to carve out a structure for herself that would allow her both to stay at the top of development and to have time for her family. This isn't about being a woman, but about having any other life than the collective Microsoft goal.

To do this she had to gear herself to a higher level of intense creativity than she thought possible. She has had to be constantly strategic and to be constantly aware of the balance of her position.

GETTING YOURSELF HEARD

One of the most difficult aspects of negotiating with family is getting everyone to listen to each other. As time goes by we develop ways of communicating with each other that we can't even see. My daughter said to me one day, 'You know we often hold two different conversations with each other at the same time. You're saying one thing and I'm saying another and it can go on for five minutes!' We laughed.

Now that we know we do it, we always catch ourselves, sometimes we just let it go on because it is funny or it is working. But it wouldn't work if we had something serious to discuss. There is attention, but it is too disjointed. Some couples have a racquet they play all the time whereby one nags and the other defends – it is just what they do. They usually solve the issues, but to an outsider listening in it looks unbalanced and it probably is.

Getting heard is one of the most difficult skills for most people. One of my clients has just been hired as the chair for the Low Pay Commission in the UK. Apart from his skills as a negotiator and his experience with trade unions and universities, he brings to the position a very clear voice of authority. He understands that people need to be heard in meetings and sees that everyone has a voice. When he judges the time is right, he sums up what he wants out of what each person has said and delivers the result. In this way, everyone feels they have had their say; there is something of each one of them in the result. 'I'm not creative,' he says, 'but I know how to sum up people's opinions and form them into something they all want to hear.'

We keep too many heartfelt wishes buried under our exterior, believing no one will want to hear them or that these heartfelt wishes are out of line with our chosen career or life path. 'If I told my company this I would be out of a job,' I am told. Just how much are you prepared to keep buried, you need to ask yourself.

For most of my life I haven't spoken out in public. When I was five I was locked in my room for a week because I lopped the top off a pathway of red tulips with my French Canadian twin friends. My friends got a scolding, I lost my freedom. The message was clear. Don't do anything that stands out or you will be stifled. I didn't find any allies either so I had to submit.

My father's back stooped and he was apologetic. 'You know I can't go against your mother.' My sister, eight years old and much better behaved, gave me a hard time all week, brought my food and displayed her freedom. I longed to be heard but my mother wouldn't listen. She wouldn't even come into my room. How can you talk to someone who isn't there? For years I wrote what I wanted to say, for magazines, newspapers, even sometimes to my husband when I couldn't get him to understand.

When I did my Sloan Fellowship in my mid-forties, I had to get up and make business presentations. The first time I presented an operations management strategy, the only person in the class I didn't like went for me. He knew I wasn't too hot on numbers and asked me to explain them in detail. I paused, in some panic. Did he really want to know or was he just gunning for me? I decided it was the latter and passed it back to him. 'How would you explain it?' I asked. The class laughed. He tried again, with more of a barb. One of the class called out, 'Don't you know an ace when you see one?' I was hooked on public speaking.

Standing there in black-stockinged feet, a small pleated skirt and huge polo-neck sweater, the student-style clothes I was having such fun wearing in my mid-career sabbatical, I decided I wanted to do more of this. When I got back to my desk a new friend slipped a drawing of a smilie face in front of me with congratulations written on it. Getting heard. What an elixir. Forty-two years on from being shut in my room, I had recovered.

On my client's lists of ten unachieved ideas (see Chapter Seven) there is almost always one about getting heard. A futures broker wants to be a film critic, a marketing executive wants to help the silent in Africa. There are many forms but they all add up to the same thing, wanting to be heard on something they are interested in or care about.

CLEAN LISTENING

The best way to have a discussion on a serious life-topic is to set in a process I call *Clean Listening*. There is a process and a format that allows both sides, or everyone if more than two, to say what they want without being hounded or side-lined. You start by agreeing a time for the discussion, say tomorrow night at eight- thirty. You put in a duration, a frame/structure around the discussion, perhaps thirty minutes. You then give each other an agreed amount of time each, you might both start off with five minutes. This five minutes is your time to say what you want to get across, without interruption. The other person has to listen, without judging or interrupting, suggesting or disagreeing.

You will find it quite startling how much better you hear someone when you do not interrupt. The person speaking gets less defensive because there are no buts and if only yous, and as they speak they get clearer and clearer and closer to what they want to say. There is respect on both sides and neither side can play the usual games.

You can vary the lengths of the time. If you have only one minute each, a time I give people in my classrooms, you will be astonished at how clearly you can say what you want in two or three sentences. Of course, the less you say, the more someone will hear you. You may want to set in three sets of five minutes, then several sets of two minutes. The longer times get the problem or idea out in the open, and the shorter times can be used for working out how to handle the issue.

When you re-negotiate with your family apply the same technique. What do they want you to be doing with them next year, in the next ten years? This way you can quickly find out their needs and plans. The more you know about these the better, as is shown in the sailing example above. What we often do when we feel pressure from our families is avoid the issue, put off the decision, hoping it will go away.

The more you get these balance issues out in the open the freer the discussion will be and the less often anyone will take an intransigent position. When we aren't heard we harden into our positions and we can barely be winkled out. It is a bit like the oyster and the pearl. People are irritated by something no one will let them have and they grow wonderful private pearls. The trouble is they have sunk themselves all the way to the bottom of the sea in their fury or resentment at not being listened to, so the pearls just never see the light of day. After a while the people carrying the yearning are long past being able to get it out themselves and they carry it as a permanent regret. What a waste.

Using this Clean Listening process helps negotiations with families because it opens responsibilities on both sides, just as it does with company and employee. When you handle your negotiations in this way, in a series of discussions, planned and timed, you also, without having to explain the point, introduce the concept and build a new kind of alliance.

If you view this Clean Listening process as an ongoing and exciting way of building new plans between you and your family, you can bring in many new ways of moving on to new futures. So many separations and divorces come because there is no mechanism for this kind of discussion. 'But he knows how I feel,' I hear, 'he is my husband.'

No, he doesn't know. You haven't given him, in an acceptable, non-threatening form, the chance to hear you. Let the pearl out of the shell. Talk now. Clean Listening is a lot simpler than the divorce court. It is a lot cheaper, too. And it is a lot more fun. The pearl shines more if you wear it as a ring that you design together than it does hidden in your murky dark.

CHAPTER FOURTEEN

BALANCING YOUR TIME

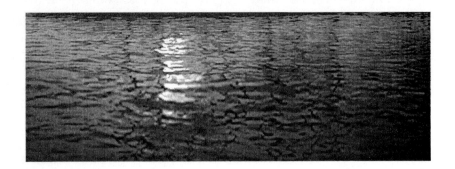

Change the habit patterns you have developed about the structure of your week. Start to restructure your week now and you can move gradually towards achieving the balance of time you want in your life. Introduce the new plans at staggered times, keeping the whole length of your life in view.

Let's look first at what can be achieved in restructuring your week, your year and your life and then see how to go about doing it. A good example is one of the human resource directors at Levi Strauss. Her husband came home one day and said he was moving his business to a small town in another state. She gasped. She loved her job working with one of the central groups at Levi's, in their very comfortable, open-culture head office in waterside San Francisco. However, she saw that this was important for his business and she went to tell Levi's that she was leaving. They gasped.

Levi's did not want to lose her. They sat down to work out a solution and came up with a structure that would allow her input and her commitment to her husband. For two years she worked one week in San Francisco and one week in her office at home in this small town. 'I loved the arrangement,' she says, 'and would have gone on doing it but my husband moved the business back to San Francisco. I had a wonderful balance between small town life and the big international city.'

What allowed her this flexibility was that her group really needed her expertise and support during a time of change they were going through. And this is valuable to remember. When you want to restructure your time in a radical way such as this, you need to look around to see where you are most valuable to your company.

A man at director level in one of the inter-governmental banks in Washington flew in to work with me on his life-strategy. He was with me for two and a half days and we worked together intensely through that time. He was, at first, quite shocked when I explained he would need to restructure his life. All he could see after thirty years in one organisation was that particular structure or something very similar or nothing at all.

Once we had decided on a Multi-Channel Life for him (see Chapter Ten) we were able to start structuring the new channels into a progressive new thirty-year future. He gradually began to see that it was true that he has as long a time ahead to structure as he had already worked. We took the channels he had decided on and put them into an drawing similar to the simple illustration opposite.

When you start to build a visual structure, with the time-scales set in, you can relax about the new beginnings you have planned in the future. You have starting dates and you have these balanced with the finishing date of the activity in which you are currently involved.

Try this for yourself. Draw in the new avenues you have decided to pursue a the chart such as the one below. Put a time-scale down one side, for the amount of years you want to chart your time. Then decide when you want to start each of the channels. For instance, you may want to be doing something in twenty years that you do not even want to begin until five years from now.

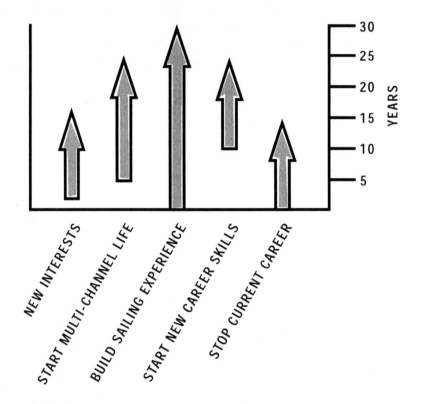

You may realise in doing this exercise that you want to finish something you are doing now much sooner than you thought. Play around with the possibilities until you think you have the right balance of old and new.

Having set in the long-term structure, it's time to look at your week and your year. We hold beliefs about the structure of our working week that started at school. The habit of turning up at the same place at the same time every morning was dinned into us before we could decide for ourselves. As we went through life we kept seeing all the people who get on buses and trains and undergrounds every day and we came to believe that that is what most of us are doing. We yearn for something else but think we have to wither to conform or drop out, win or be a loser, succeed in the hierarchy or be something 'creative' like an artist.

It is also guilt that keeps us in the seven o'clock on Monday morning to seven o'clock on Friday night pattern. It is actually more difficult to break our own habit patterns than it is to convince those around us that we would like to.

A simple way of breaking the day-to-day structure initially is to offer your services to an arts body or something similar, making sure it is a body your company wants to be seen to be supporting. Then you have permission to create a wedge of non-office time during your actual working week.

List out all the activities in which you are involved in your week and put a percentage on the time you want to spend on each of them. If you go over one hundred per cent, think again; you are probably running to keep up. Balancing your time isn't a question of doing more and more better, it is seeing you have the elements there that will give you the success you want.

When I looked at this issue with Prue Leith, I ploughed happily through her diary. I kept asking her, 'How much use will this appointment be to what you want to do in two years time, in five years time?' 'But I've always done these things,' she argued. I was fairly ruthless, 'If you don't throw out some of the old stuff where are you going to put the new stuff?'

If you are ever in a meeting thinking, 'This is a waste of my time,' then you need to cut this responsibility out, pass it to someone else. What you want in your diary are only those things you know will achieve the results you want. Balancing time isn't just pushing elements of your life around and around.

Measure the amount of time you put into each meeting or piece of work and see if it balances with the success you achieve from it. Be ruthless with yourself and you will have more time to play with in your time equation.

Probably the most important element of your week is your quiet time. You may have to move it but it is a constant segment of your day, a time you never leave out. It is when you are at your most creative and strategic, so factor it in first.

If you are moving towards a Multi-Channel Life, start to restructure gradually. It is still early days for building successful alliances between companies and people working outside them, and too many people are finding the transition difficult. These people find themselves either on the inside or on the outside. You have to understand that you need to know more about this than your company does and that it is your responsibility, if you want to work this way to show your company how these possibilities might operate.

Take it step by step. Start, for instance, by taking some project work home for a day or so a week. Find another person who wants to move towards a new structure and see if you can, between you, figure out how both of you doing this could save your company some money. Offer to share an office, share a secretary, show some creative benefit to the company. Ease your way into the new structure. The future starts now on this; what you begin today you can build on tomorrow.

TOOLS

- First, put in that quiet time like a band through every day. You may have to move it but it is always a segment of your day.

- Leave at least a half-day of clear diary for the unexpected.

- Put in something new, such as being a voluntary advisor to an arts organisation, which will break the pattern of your every day.

- Ruthlessly cut out the old stuff.

- Measure the amount of time you put in against the success you achieve. Cut out anything that doesn't balance.

- Find someone else who wants to restructure in a similar way and offer this as a financial or bottom-line benefit to the company.

CHAPTER FIFTEEN

STAYING IN BALANCE

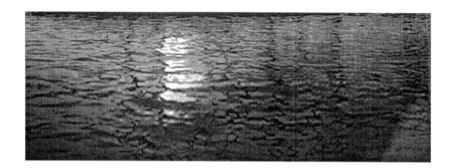

This chapter is the quick-reference section of the book. Having worked your way through the stages of building a new balance into your life, here is a step-by-step reminder to keep you there. This covers managing the transition time when you are in the phase between the old ways and the new, as well as the practical 'to do' issues, in the form of a check list so that you can check in and out when you need to.

WHAT TO DO WHILE YOU'RE IN TRANSITION

Transition is necessarily a time of uncertainty. Acknowledge this and live with it, not against it. If you don't have uncertainty, you will only get more of the same and make no worthwhile changes. Some of the most powerful people I know have the ability to live with uncertainty, and the humility to acknowledge it publicly. The less strong try to hide it because it makes them feel insecure and exposed.

When I worked with an executive board member of an international oil company, he at first showed all the poise and security of someone who had been in the same industry and only two companies for thirty years. He knew his world. He came to me to decide whether to stay on for a few more years or leave. He had absolutely no idea what else he might do if he left, other than golf and travel.

I found out that he was a very good chairman at meetings; he knew how to stay in the uncertain and reel everyone in at the appropriate time. He admitted quite freely that since starting to work with me he had started to feel very unsure of himself. Good, I told him, just stay there, we'll have you on to some new directions within a few sessions.

From time to time he would ask when we would stop opening up possibilities and fine-tune to a structured new direction. I knew that he was uneasy being unsure, out of kilter. I asked for patience and got it. In return he gained new openings, he didn't fall into the trap so many retiring people do of getting bored or just finding some similar work again.

By giving himself this transition time, he was able to explore new aspects of his relationships with his wife and children. He worked his way towards a new balance in his life, step by step, without rushing ahead, even though moving fast was what he more comfortably knew, and the transition was busy, challenging and happily new.

DON'T SLIP ON THE FEAR PATCH

I have already written about fear, but it is important to consider at this point because when you are in transition fear is one of the major factors you have to deal with. One of my clients, who came to work with me on a one-to-one basis after attending one of my lectures, was a very successful investment banker in his forties. When he came for the first session, he said the reason he had decided to work with me was because of the relief he felt when I had talked openly about fear.

It was the first time, he said, that anyone in his life had said fear of change was quite normal. He said that fear had kept him from making a new career move for almost ten years. When I smiled and told him that fear always comes up when we are stuck, changing or out of balance, that everyone has it, he burst out laughing with the joy of not feeling isolated anymore. Knowing that there will be times of fear helps. Not facing the fear means you are more likely to slip on a patch of it.

CHECKING IN, CHECKING OUT: STAYING IN BALANCE

Check One: Find a Partner to Work with

Find a friend who is also going through this period of life-balancing change and follow through the period of transition together. This person should be outside your family. Set in regular times to talk and meet. Be absolutely open and frank with this person, sharing successes and failures. Meet somewhere outside your usual surroundings so that that place is particular to the transition period. Make it a pleasant place so that you want to be there, perhaps a wonderful bar with comfortable seats or a walk by the river in summer. It isn't a good idea to use your office because there are all the old signals going on there, nor your home for the same reasons. Setting aside a defined time and a clear agenda ensures you come away having progressed as well as having shared your experiences.

Check Two: Check Your Lists and Visuals

Look at the lists and visuals you have done while you were reading through the programme, every Monday morning, at the same time as you start and plan your work week. Look at them again every Friday evening as you wind up your office week. Never leave them out through lack of time; you deserve to be given the same attention as you give your work life. This is your story you are dealing with.

Check Three: Measure Your Health

Make sure that you are keeping up your health. It is no use just having it on your plan. Unless you are bounding with health, it isn't enough. Unless you can feel the energy streaming through your body when you stretch in the morning, you aren't aware enough of your body and what it needs. Check your health every week. When one of the points isn't measuring up to expectations, bring it up to the top of the list and focus on it. For instance, you may have missed certain foods you need, or not gone for the mountain hike you scheduled in. Reschedule it as a priority; put those foods on your list.

Check Four: Be Your Own Observer
Never feel bad about not doing something that takes you out of balance. See your new balance as a new way of understanding the changing world you live in and your best place in it. See it as a way of getting to know yourself better, watching for what you do and don't do, a way of observing and then teaching yourself on an ongoing basis to keep yourself in balance. Know that now you have set in your guidelines you can very quickly change and adapt to any turbulence, change of direction or opportunity.

Check Five: Keep the Rings around Your Soul in Play
If you start to feel overwhelmed and worry that the world is getting on top of you, go to the heart of achieving balance – your soul and the rings around your soul. You will recognise this central place of comfort that allows you to be your strongest. Look quickly at the whole spectrum of your life – through all the layers, from the inner you to the outer you, right through to where you fit in the global picture. When you think quickly of yourself in this connected way you regain the highest confidence levels and the toughest resilience whatever the situation.

Check Six: Play Like a Child and Support a Life-Long Strategy
Remember that the further you look ahead, the more time you allow yourself to plan all the things you want to include in your life. Look back often at a childhood time when you were at your happiest and play your current circumstance with the same natural sense of well-being.

Check Seven: Accentuate Bravery, Courage and Heart
In these three key words you have the three core qualities you need to centre a balanced life.

Check Eight: Dance Your Balance, Continue Your Quiet Time
Always be aware of the universe's giant holding pattern in which you are

such a precisely placed part. Never forget that your role in this ongoing dance is the same role as all the other parts – to move forward, change, grow and be a part of the dance. Keep your quiet time every day, the time that reminds you of who you are and where you want to be.

Check Nine: Read Your Face

Keep a watch on your face. Look at yourself in the mirror several times a day. This is not vanity. It's a practical way of seeing how you feel. Your face is your quickest reference point. If you look pinched or your face looks long, you are out of balance and you need to do something to change your situation. Something very simple may make the difference. If you let some space into your body quickly you will immediately feel a lot better; try some relaxing breathing, a few yoga stretches, a walk. If these are not enough then go back to the section of the programme that you need to be reminded of. If you see a broad clear face you know you are OK.

Check Ten: Check Your Aliveness

Ask yourself each morning why you are glad to be alive. When a counsellor friend in Seattle asked me to do this I started to talk about all the knowledge I had gained in my travels. She just looked at me, 'Is that why you are glad to be alive?' It took me a week of asking the same question of myself until I got to the simpler things of life, such as: yesterday I saw the most beautiful, sweet-smelling Chilean jasmine; this morning when I got out of bed I was thinking of my daughter and the hug we gave each other when she went home last night; at lunch-time I talked to a friend in Australia and we laughed at the same things. It took me a month to realise that the best reason I have to be glad I am alive is my sense of aliveness. It is the feeling I have when my heart is steady, my head is quiet and my emotions are focused on joy. I can't always have this. But, based on my better and better balancing skills, I know I can have it progressively more and more often and I do.